*James E. Hightower Jr., EdD*
*Editor*

# Caring for People from Birth to Death

*More pre-publication*
*REVIEWS, COMMENTARIES, EVALUATIONS . . .*

"**T**his book provides pastors with an excellent map of the emotional, social, and spiritual issues facing parishioners at each stage of life. A quick read before any pastoral visit will refresh your mind about psychosocial spiritual issues and stage-appropriate interventions.

It is particularly helpful in identifying the spiritual needs and experiences at each stage of development. An excellent quick reference to the human condition for time-strapped pastors."

**Andrew D. Lester, PhD**
*Professor of Pastoral Theology
and Pastoral Counseling,
Texas Christian University,
Fort Worth*

"**T**his book helped me review the entire process of my own life as a person, a husband, a father, and a minister. It was like a shot of adrenaline! The contributors give attention to spiritual growth in each stage of the life cycle with the assumption that we never finish the process.

The book is itself an example of Christian care just for the way it treats the reader. It revealed to me so many ways I could have done better in my own life, but it left me cared for."

**Myron C. Madden, PhD**
*Consultant,
The McFarland Institute,
New Orleans, Louisiana*

The Haworth Pastoral Press
An Imprint of The Haworth Press, Inc.

# Caring for People from Birth to Death

# Caring for People from Birth to Death

James E. Hightower Jr., EdD
Editor

The Haworth Pastoral Press
An Imprint of The Haworth Press, Inc.
New York • London • Oxford

$\frac{2}{0}1$

Published by

The Haworth Pastoral Press, an imprint of The Haworth Press, Inc., 10 Alice Street, Binghamton, NY 13904-1580

Cover design by Marylouise E. Doyle.

**Library of Congress Cataloging-in-Publication Data**

Caring for people from birth to death / James E. Hightower Jr. [editor]. — Rev. and enlarged ed.

Xi, 204 p. cm. Originally published as :

Rev. ed. of: Caring for folks from birth to death. Nashville, Tenn. : Broadman Press, 1985.
Includes bibliographical references and index.
ISBN 0-7890-0571-9 (alk. paper)
1. Pastoral psychology. I. Hightower, James E. II. Hightower, James E. Caring for people from birth to death.
BV4012.C319  1999
253—dc21                                                                          98-47910
                                                                                              CIP

# CONTENTS

# ABOUT THE EDITOR

**James E. Hightower, EdD,** is Director of the Pastoral Counseling Division of the McFarland Institute in New Orleans, Louisiana. Currently, Dr. Hightower also serves as adjunct faculty member of Our Lady of Holy Cross College and at the University of New Orleans in the Counselor Education Program. He is a consultant in pastoral care in all fifty states, training pastors in marriage counseling skills, hospital ministry, grief ministry, and other pastoral care skills. In addition, Dr. Hightower was the editor of *Proclaim* from 1980 to 1986. His articles have been published in *Home Life, Baptist Program, Christian Singles, Living with Preschoolers, Living with Teenagers, Mature Living, The Door, The Theological Educator of New Orleans Baptist Seminary, The Journal of Pastoral Care,* and *Friends Journal.* Dr. Hightower is also the author of *Voices from the Old Testament; Called to Care: Helping People Through Pastoral Care; Preaching That Heals;* and *Pastoral Preaching for Hurting People;* compiler of *Illustrating the Gospel of Matthew* and *Illustrating Paul's Letter to the Romans;* and co-author of *After They Join.*

# Contributors

**Cos H. Davis Jr., EdD,** has expressed his sense of calling in many ways. He has served as a pastor, a seminary professor in early childhood education, a leader in his denomination in the development of early childhood materials for church use, a teacher of children and parents, and a pastoral counselor. He currently works as a pastoral counselor and family educator through his privately operated ministry, Family Resource Services.

**George H. Gaston III, PhD,** is the Director of Spiritual Development and Community Outreach with the Memorial Hermann Healthcare System in Houston, Texas. Most of his ministry years have been spent in local church pastoral ministry. Holding pastorates in Texas and Louisiana has equipped him to speak to the practical ministry issues addressed in this book. For several years, George served as an assistant professor of pastoral ministry at Southwestern Baptist Theological Seminary. Before coming to his present position, he had been pastor of the Pioneer Drive Baptist Church in Abilene, Texas for over five years, and pastor of the Willow Meadows Baptist Church in Houston for ten years.

**Albert L. Meiburg, PhD,** began his teaching career on a college campus, later becoming a hospital chaplain for eighteen years. He has served on the faculties of Crozer Theological Seminary, Colgate Rochester Divinity School, and Southeastern Baptist Theological Seminary. In retirement he is a part-time professor of pastoral care at the Divinity Schools of Gardner-Webb and Campbell Universities in North Carolina. Al's special interest in ministry with older adults is reflected in his chapter.

**Thom Meigs, PhD,** is Minister of Pastoral Care and Wellness and Supervisor of the Counseling Ministry of Park Cities Baptist Church, Dallas, Texas. He served eighteen years as a seminary professor of pastoral care and counseling, four years as a college chaplain, three years as a hospital chaplain, and ten years as a pastor in Kentucky, Virginia, and Florida. Thom brings an accumulation of experience with his own young adult children and special insight to the young adult years.

**James L. Minton, EdD,** is the Associate Pastor/Counselor at Immanuel Baptist Church in Little Rock, Arkansas. For eighteen years, he was the youth education professor at New Orleans Baptist Theological Seminary. He is a Licensed Professional Counselor, Clinical Member of the American Association for Marriage and Family Therapy, and a charter member of the American Association of Christian Counselors. Jim brings his experience as a youth minister, professor, and counselor to this work.

**Bruce P. Powers, PhD,** has served as a staff minister in churches, was Director of the Church Program Training Center for the Baptist Sunday school board, and since 1977 has been a seminary professor. He is currently Associate Dean of the Campbell University Divinity School, Buies Creek, NC, and Langston Professor of Christian Education and Congregational Studies.

**Bruce Powers Jr., PhD,** has a master's degree in developmental psychology from the University of Notre Dame. He is currently serving as a minister to children and is a student in the Campbell University Divinity School.

# Preface

Fifteen years ago, the first edition of this book, titled *Caring for Folks from Birth to Death,* was published. One year later, the Spanish edition was released. Both editions have been highly successful, for which I am grateful. In the first edition, I said:

> As I have traveled around the United States leading pastoral care workshops, I sensed a gap in the pastoral care literature. Ministers need a concise handbook that will help them quickly grasp the developmental issues that persons face and give them some ideas of how the church can effectively minister to these folks. (p. 5)

I believe this gap in the literature still exists today.

I am delighted with this revised and enlarged edition. Although updated, the first two sections of each chapter remain the same as in the first edition. The first section helps you understand the developmental issues people face. The second helps you understand what is appropriate ministry to people, based on their developmental task. In addition, a third section has been added concerning how spirituality grows and declines in different eras of a person's life.

The original group of authors joined me in this revision.

An effort was made to leave each contributor's style intact. Also, the contributors included a bibliography of additional resources not referred to in their chapters. No attempt has been made to avoid duplication, because one minister might have a particular interest in adolescence and another in aging.

This book is offered as a tool in ministry to persons who care for others. It will give you easy access to developmental theory, practical ministry ideas, and spiritual growth. To that end we pray it is helpful.

*James E. Hightower Jr.*
*New Orleans, Louisiana*

Chapter 1

# The Preschool Years: Foundations for Life

Cos H. Davis Jr.

Several years ago, in a church where I served as pastor, a young child drew a picture of me. The picture showed me standing behind the pulpit, gesturing with one hand in the air. I was obviously preaching! I was startled to think that the young child's only perception of me was the activity he saw me doing most often. But his experiences were limited, and as he got to know me in other relationships, his perception broadened.

The same holds true of the clergy's many ministers' perceptions of preschoolers—children who have not yet reached age five. Our ideas about them are often based on fragments of knowledge and experience. As we learn more through reading, observing, and experience, our understanding of them increases. As our understanding of preschoolers grows, we will be able to minister to them more effectively.

This chapter is designed to help broaden our understanding of preschoolers. Why are preschool years considered foundational? What are a preschooler's developmental tasks? Can a preschooler learn about God? How do preschoolers learn? What are some basic needs of preschoolers? What are some practical ways a minister can relate to preschoolers?

## PRESCHOOL YEARS ARE FOUNDATIONAL

The first five years of life are highly significant. What children learn and feel during this time, particularly about themselves, will

*1*

be foundational to the rest of their life. By the time a child turns five, he or she should have a pretty good idea as to his or her worth to parents and other important people such as teachers. A child will have acquired some basic feelings about what parents believe is important. If children can be helped to feel good about themselves, a good foundation for relationships with others can be built.

The preschool years are an excellent opportunity to lay the foundation for a child's spiritual life. This foundation is important for Christian conversion and spiritual growth. Good learning experiences at church are a great place to start.

Christian conversion and growth do not happen in a vacuum. The person who makes a willful choice to receive Christ as Savior does so out of a background of experiences that have prepared him or her for this decision. The better job we do in the preschool years, the better the child will be able to relate positively to God.

The men and women in our churches who teach preschoolers are doing important work! They, along with parents, are building the foundation necessary for Christian conversion and growth. There is a real sense that a preschool teacher is just as involved in a person's conversion as the children's, youth, or adult teacher who actually leads him or her to accept Christ at a later time. Paul wrote in 1 Corinthians 3:6, "I planted, Apollos watered, but God was giving the increase" (NASB).[1]

## The Needs of a Preschooler

Your work with people has proven that they act or react according to some need in their lives. Often, people do not know why they do what they do or say what they say. A need, though unrecognized, still clamors for attention. God has made us with certain needs—some of which can be met only in relation to others.

Preschoolers have needs, too. Understanding what those needs are and how to meet them will enable you to minister more effectively to children and, in turn, help parents and teachers meet their needs.

### Love

Love is the most basic need of preschoolers. They sense they are loved as adults express gentleness and patience in relation to their physical needs and their inability to do many things for themselves. Loving a preschooler means doing what is best for him or her. Loving means understanding the child enough to know what is best and being willing and unselfish enough to meet the child's needs. Proverbs 22:6 says, "Train up a child in the way he should go; and when he is old, he will not depart from it" (KSV). Loving a child means taking responsibility to guide his or her life in ways that will help the child be a well-adjusted, contributing member of society and servant of God. The attitude of such love is expressed in the words of Sybil Waldrop, "Every child needs someone who is just crazy about him."[2]

## Self-Worth

Preschoolers need to know that they are important to people who are important to them. They learn to value themselves only as those closest to them treat them as persons of worth. If this need is satisfied, they will learn that others are valuable too. The child's future, in terms of relationships, basically hinges on whether or not he or she feels important to significant people. Such a sense of self-worth is not taught through a relentless barrage of gifts or the absence of rules or regulations, but by the kind of love that deals patiently and purposefully with the needs of the child.

## Acceptance

Love is expressed and self-worth is taught as preschoolers sense that they are accepted by significant adults. Children need to know they are wanted and deeply appreciated by others. Parents must consciously attempt to instill the feeling that they are proud of their child and that the child does not have to do anything to be loved. Children are loved because of who they are, not because of what they do! Before a child is born, some parents need to be helped to accept the child as a gift from God and be happy if the Lord gives them a daughter instead of a son or vice versa.

## Trust

Preschoolers are almost totally dependent on adults to meet their basic physical, emotional, social, and spiritual needs. A baby learns trust by the way he or she is cared for—if hunger and comfort needs are met in a loving manner. Young children need to be assured through experience that they can depend on their parents and teachers to meet their needs and do what is best for them. The words "Johnny, I love you" are confusing to Johnny if his parents or teachers say the words but do not meet his needs.

A young child's sense of trust is also a good foundation for faith in God. Without trust, faith in God is more difficult. There are several biblical references of Jesus' use of family relationships to describe the believer's relationship to God (Matthew 5:9; 6:6, 8-9; 7:8-11). Such verses emphasize that appropriate trusting relationships with the Heavenly Father are fostered in the context of trusting relationships in the earthly home!

## Security

Preschoolers need to feel safe. Apart from proper care, they can get into some dangerous situations. They may put something unsafe in their mouth or try to put the end of an object in an electrical outlet. They may climb on top of a table or chair. They need adults who will recognize the limitations of their judgment and will do whatever is necessary to keep them as safe as possible.

Parents and teachers who set limits to protect the preschooler are building the child's sense of security as well as an appreciation for some rules. However, caution should be used so as not to stifle every attempt to do something new. Also, judgment should be used so as not to protect the child from the minor scrapes that come as a part of normal play activities. If the parent or teacher is too protective, the preschooler will feel scared to try anything new! Balance is the key!

## Guidance

Preschoolers do not come with an understanding of how to get along in a world of people and things. This means they must be taught by parents and teachers. Guidance for the preschooler should involve: (1) teaching the child the proper use of toys and other objects without hurting himself or herself or others, or destroying the object; (2) teaching the child to gradually become more concerned for the rights and needs of others. This is quite difficult with young children who focus primarily on their own needs. However, by the fourth or fifth year, children should be able to play cooperatively with others and "take turns" with the use of toys. Meeting other needs related to self-image and love helps free the child to be more cooperative and focus less on what the child wants.

*Independence*

Growing preschoolers need to develop a sense of independence within their capabilities. Of course, some things are well beyond their limits, both mentally and physically. Parents and teachers need to be aware of the child's limitations so as not to frustrate him or her with a task that is too difficult. To be able to do this one must understand that preschoolers are not "little adults" and cannot reason as adults. However, there are many things preschoolers can do, want to do, and should be allowed to do for themselves.

## How a Preschooler Thinks

Several years ago while teaching a seminary course on child development, a student related how his son had come home from school without his cap. The father threatened him by saying, "If you do that again, I'll knock your head off!" The next day, his son came home with two caps—his and someone else's! This story illustrates some of the characteristics of thinking of young children—they take you literally, and morals do not seem to influence their conscious thought.

*Literal Minded*

It is often amusing to get the interpretation of the mature five-year-old's understanding of what we say. On a trip with my family I called my five-year-old daughter's attention to a huge bridge up ahead by saying, "Kristen, we're going over that bridge in a little while." Her reaction was unusual excitement—she could hardly believe it! When we crossed the bridge she expressed her disappointment by complaining, "Daddy, we didn't go over that bridge." She had understood me literally to say we were going over the top of the bridge!

This limitation of literal-mindedness often causes confusion to the young child and should alert us to speak in more precise terms. While we cannot divest ourselves of all the "language of Zion," some terminology is particularly confusing to the young child. Remember how the literal-minded child thinks when he or she hears such statements as "Jesus lives in my heart" or the words of favorite hymns such as "There Is a Fountain Filled with Blood!"

## Here and Now

The preschooler is limited to the here and now. If you ask a five-year-old to describe God, he or she may (if at that stage of capability) draw a very large stick person. As adults, we realize that God is a spirit (John 4:24) and cannot be adequately described in human terms. But preschoolers have no concept of a spirit and describe everything according to their experience. For example, a preschooler who has seen only a blue ball may not think that a ball can be red. Therefore, the red ball is not a ball! He or she must be told that it is.

## Short Attention Span

To some adults, one of the most frustrating things about preschoolers is their inability to pay attention for an extended period of time. This is one reason why preschoolers learn best through a variety of short-term activities. The parent or teacher who insists on a two-year-old sitting still for five minutes while they tell a long Bible story will not have an audience after about a minute or so! Therefore, teaching activities and materials must be designed with consideration for the short attention span of preschoolers.

## Shallow Learner

Preschoolers also tend to be interested only in the shallow or surface facts of an object or story. They cannot deal with the subtle meanings or implications of a story such as the "Good Samaritan." Only the simplest facts can be related. Likewise, a child looking at a nature object may be impressed with only the color and size of the object while seeming unconcerned with other characteristics. This is why it is important not to expect a preschooler to be able to deal with great detail or intricate facts. The preschooler must be exposed to the same object, song, or story many times before he or she will tire of it. Why? Because as shallow learners, preschoolers gradually understand more and more through repeated exposure.

## Saying and Understanding

One final point needs to be made relative to the thinking of the preschooler. Preschoolers can say many things they do not understand. Their physical ability to say complicated words or words with religious significance may be far advanced of their ability to understand what they are saying. For example, a child can be taught to say, "Jesus lives in my heart" and that sounds religious and spiritual. But, does the preschooler really understand the truth of that statement? Can a preschooler really put that truth to use? We must not assume that saying something spiritual means the preschooler has understood what the word or phrase means.

## A PRESCHOOLER'S DEVELOPMENTAL TASKS

During the first five years of life an individual is confronted with three basic psychosocial tasks. Erik Erikson identified these developmental tasks as trust, autonomy, and initiative.[3] If these tasks do not begin at the proper time, it is doubtful the person will make the proper life adjustments at the other stages of life. For example, the developmental tasks of adolescence and adulthood are related to those of the earliest years. Should a person be deficient in trust, autonomy, and initiative, his or her psychosocial growth at later stages would be adversely affected.

Now, let's overview the developmental tasks of preschoolers to show the importance of each one. Each task is discussed with a general time frame in focus, although every child will not fit this time frame precisely because of differences in physical, emotional, and mental maturation.

## Trust

Trust is the first and most basic developmental task in life. Trust is learning to rely on others for needs to be met. It is learning the feeling of security and well-being about your relationship with significant others.

This task has its roots in the first two years of life when the child is most dependent. It arises out of the fact that almost everything must be done for the young child during this time. Young children cannot feed, change, bathe, or cover themselves. These are the concerns of the parent or other caregiver. If children learn that others are going to take care of them, they can "relax" and trust the parent or caregiver. If a child's basic needs are met in a loving way, he or she will develop a basic sense of trust.

## Autonomy

Some refer to autonomy as the understanding that you are a person apart from others. You have a self of your own. You are independent of others. This task depends on trust and is a focus of the two- and three-year-old child. Autonomy is often expressed in many types of independent actions.

During the first two years of life children gradually develop skills that will make them less dependent on adults to do many things for them. By around one year they are beginning to walk, and by eighteen months or so, they begin to talk. These skills are pretty well developed by the time a child reaches two. These skills, along with feeding themselves and toilet training, will be further refined by the time they reach their fourth birthday.

Perhaps you have heard parents refer to their child as a "terrible two." The reference is usually to a child who is at the emotional stage of having a tantrum when he or she does not get his or her way or becomes frustrated with an activity. This is a normal expression for children who are trying to establish independence and are frustrated by the restraints of adults or by an activity that is too difficult for their abilities.

While the years of autonomy or independence can be trying for adults, all is not negative. These are years of learning for children, testing their skills, and gaining confidence. They are growing and feel safe enough to try out new things on their own. Parents who will deal patiently with their child during this difficult stage will see emerge a more confident and self-assured individual.

### Initiative

The four- or five-year-old is at the age when initiative becomes important. While the twos or threes expressed independence within their limited abilities, fours and fives have more abilities and use their imagination quite well.

Fours and fives act upon their environment to change it. Give a five-year-old a set of wooden blocks and he or she might build a house with doors and windows! Their imaginations are active and they use them to draw or paint, or in other creative expressions. While they still mix fantasy and reality, their initiative finds expression in some form.

During this stage, they need lots of opportunity to express themselves through music, art, stories, blocks, and so forth. They are totally involved and approach their work with intensity and abandon!

## CAN A PRESCHOOLER LEARN ABOUT GOD?

What an important question for a pastor or minister of education! The answer to this question has all kinds of interesting implications about whether to provide "baby-sitting" or planned learning experiences while preschoolers are at church. The answer to this question also has implications related to whether just "anyone" can work with preschoolers or whether we need knowledgeable, trained people to teach them. This question also opens for consideration the provision of well-equipped rooms, adequate space, and learning materials appropriate for preschoolers.

To say that preschoolers are interested in learning is an understatement. They are consumed by the need to learn. They investigate almost anything that will stand still for an examination! Preschoolers unleash a relentless barrage of questions about what? why? who? Adults are often amazed at their untiring energy as they go from one activity to another and then on to another. What is all the ceaseless activity about? Why the compulsion to get on with living?

## *Learning*

Preschoolers are learners. They are acquiring bits and pieces of ideas that will later become concepts. They are acquiring feelings that they will later associate with facts. To say that a preschooler cannot learn would be nonsense. We know they learn.

But can preschoolers learn about God? Can foundational feelings and ideas be taught as building blocks for later years? Should we wait until the elementary school years to begin teaching children about God?

## *Avenues of Learning*

Preschoolers can learn about God. God wants to make Himself known to the young as well as to those who are older, through whatever means they can know Him. The following are tested avenues through which preschoolers can learn about God.

## *Relationships with Significant People*

Parents, family members, and teachers provide the most important avenue through which preschoolers learn. The value of positive relationships is incalculable to the preschooler's feelings of personal value. Through relationships they learn about their self-worth as love is provided or withheld. They learn values as they are modeled by significant adults. In essence, their whole outlook on life and their concept of God are influenced by people who are important to them. Their feelings about being loved and accepted by God is greatly dependent on whether or not they feel this love and acceptance from those who mean the most to them.

## *Senses*

God made us with five senses. Preschoolers use all of these for learning. Through hearing, smelling, seeing, tasting, and touching a young child becomes familiar with the world God has made. These physical gifts are the way preschoolers deal with the world around them and offer an excellent opportunity to teach about God and his care for them.

## Repetition

Unlike adults, preschoolers do not easily tire of seeing or hearing the same thing over and over again. The fifth time the story is told can hold as much joy and excitement for the preschooler as the first. Why do preschoolers never seem to tire of the same story or song? They learn from repetition. Hearing or seeing something repeated gives them the opportunity to build on previous experience. Little by little, through repetition, the preschooler learns more about God and the people and things He has made.

## Play

Preschoolers also learn through what adults refer to as "play." Play is not a useless activity—it is a child's work. Play is his or her business. Through play, children learn about people and things in their world. They use their imaginations as they act-out the role of a policeman, nurse, father, mother, etc. Through play they experiment with ideas and gain confidence in themselves and their abilities. The play or activity approach to learning by preschool teachers allows learning to proceed from the needs and interests of children rather than imposing "learning" that is not of interest to them.

## Doing

Preschoolers are doers. They learn through participating. They are active and involved. Understanding what children are capable of doing frees parents and teachers to allow children to do what they can for themselves. Doing and accomplishing tasks builds a child's confidence and independence. Such self-confidence will encourage him or her to participate in other activities in which he or she can learn about God.

## Imitating

Preschoolers also learn by doing what they see others do. Parents and teachers can be surprised when they observe a preschooler repeat their actions or words. The fact that preschoolers learn by imitation should serve as a caution to those who teach them—exhibit only positive actions and words!

## Curiosity

The hunger to know leads preschoolers to explore what is unknown to them. Curiosity prompts them to smell, taste, and touch almost any object. They are most happy when a variety of materials are supplied for them to explore. A preschooler's natural desire to learn provides the teacher with an unbelievable opportunity to teach about God and the things He made.

## Satisfaction

Preschoolers learn to have positive feelings and attitudes about themselves if they have satisfying experiences in what they are doing. Satisfaction comes when they are able to complete a task within their own range of ability or to have positive, affirming relationships with parents and a growing degree of competence in relating to other preschoolers.

## The Bible and Preschoolers

One of the major concerns of the church is to teach the Bible to all who will avail themselves of the opportunity to learn about God's revelation through Scripture. The Bible is a book for all ages. Preschoolers can learn some important biblical concepts that are foundational to those they should learn at a later age. For this reason, those who teach preschoolers are not "baby-sitting" or entertaining preschoolers while everyone else is learning about the Bible. Preschool teachers "teach" preschoolers about the Bible.

An important consideration in teaching preschoolers the Bible is to teach it at their level of understanding. Biblical truth must be simplified and communicated in ways that preschoolers learn best. For example, singing "God made the flower. Thank you, God" to a preschooler who is examining a flower communicates a biblical truth about creation. This is an appropriate approach, but is far less complicated than discussing the stewardship implications of Genesis 1 with a group of adults. Both the preschooler and the adults are being taught at their own level of understanding. What the preschooler is being taught (that God made the world for our benefit) is foundational to the idea of stewardship that the adults are being taught!

## Biblical Concepts for Preschoolers

To clarify the idea of teaching foundational concepts, the following biblical subjects have been listed with a teaching goal for each.

*God.* We want preschoolers to have positive feelings about people and things associated with God. We want them to associate the created world with God.

*Jesus.* We want preschoolers to sense that Jesus was born, grew, belonged to a family, and was a very special person.

*Natural world.* Our aim is to teach preschoolers that God made the world good and beautiful and that "thank you, God" is an appropriate response.

*Bible.* We want to help preschoolers think of the Bible as a special book that tells about God and Jesus.

*Self.* The biblical view of the importance of oneself should be communicated to preschoolers. Personal relationships, environment, and Bible-related activities can enhance the child's appreciation of him or her self as a person of worth.

*Others.* Preschool teachers try to help preschoolers become more aware that others are important, too. With proper guidance, the preschooler should begin to act and respond to others in appropriate ways.

*Family.* We desire to help preschoolers become more aware of what God planned for families and to learn some ways in which families are special to Him.

*Church.* We want preschoolers to have good experiences at church and to have positive feelings about church.

### *HOW YOU CAN MINISTER TO PRESCHOOLERS*

There are many things you can do personally and through others to minister to the preschoolers who are a part of your congregation. The following are some practical suggestions related to the information already shared on the development and needs of preschoolers.

#### *Maximize Opportunities of Foundational Years*

As the leader of your church you have an excellent opportunity to influence parents, teachers, and church committees regarding the importance of the foundational years.

*Influence Teachers and Appropriate Committees*
*to Determine Definite Goals*
*for Teaching Preschoolers*

Working with appropriate preschool materials, committees can determine definite educational goals for each preschool stage and age. This work is usually assigned to the Preschool Committee. Teachers can receive specific training related to readiness levels of the children they teach and how to determine goals for them.

*Use Foundational Years to Relate to God's Plan*
*for Conversion and Christian Growth*

Use every opportunity to help teachers and educational committees see that God wants teachers and parents to become partners in His redemptive purpose. Parents and teachers can be helped to see that the foundational years can be used as part of the process of conversion and Christian growth. The preschool years are the time for building a trust that can become the foundation for saving faith at a later time.

*Provide a Leader Who Understands Preschoolers*
*and Is Competent in Planning*
*for Preschoolers, Parents, and Teachers*

Your church may need to designate a person (staff or volunteer) who will be responsible for planning overall programs for preschoolers. The quality of programs for preschoolers and their parents can be improved greatly when a person is specifically assigned to that task.

### Prepare Sermons and Offer Seminars on the Importance of the Foundational Years

Sermons can be prepared so that information related to the importance of the preschool years can be shared. When appropriate, occasional references to young children will communicate your love for them and support for work related to them.

### Be a Supporter of Preschool Work

One of the most helpful things you can do is to have a positive attitude toward preschoolers, parents, and the ministry of the Church related to them. An occasional supportive word about certain planned events, a verbal pat on the back to preschool workers, and an interest in what is happening will communicate that you are a friend to preschool work.

### Provide Training for Understanding Preschoolers' Needs

Many parents would be receptive to a seminar designed to help them understand and meet the needs of their preschoolers. The church needs to offer help in this area because so little of what they can read on their own is dealt with in a Christian context. The needs of preschoolers should be part of the basic content of the ongoing training program for all preschool teachers. Teachers must start with the child and his or her needs in order to be an effective teacher.

### Be Aware of How Preschoolers Think

The fact that preschoolers are literal, concrete, and shallow in their thinking has some important implications for you. What can be done to recognize this reality?

*Prepare Worship Services with Some Consideration for Preschoolers*

Make a definite attempt to communicate with young children through a sermon illustration they will understand. Occasionally choose music they can sing. Provide a children's sermon or Bible story during the worship time.

*Keep Teaching Concepts at an Appropriate Level*

Avoid being pressured by parents and others for teachers to teach concepts that are inappropriate for them. The earlier statement about teaching goals related to preschoolers should be considered. Remember that because a concept is biblical is not justification for attempting to teach it to a preschooler. There are two tests for what to teach preschoolers: (1) Is it biblical? (2) Is it appropriate for a preschooler?

The following suggestions are purely personal—things you can do with preschoolers to help them feel they are important to you.

*Eyeball to Eyeball*

As adults we have difficulty realizing how frustrating it must be to relate to people when we can only talk to their kneecaps. Get the point? You will greatly improve the preschoolers' appreciation for you, and yours for them, if you bend down to talk to them on their eye level. Look in their eyes, smile, and say something such as, "Johnny, I'm glad you're at church today." This brief contact will make a real difference in how children and their parents perceive you. If you really want to and have the time, ask parents to be sure that you get to greet the children as they leave the worship service.

*Get to Know Preschoolers*

Many pastors and staff persons spend lots of time getting to know the names, hobbies, and other facts about adult members. What about getting to know the names of preschoolers so that you can call their names when you speak to them? You might want to ask parents to make a name tag for their child to wear if you decide to greet them on a certain Sunday. This can be done several times until you have learned all their names.

### Be Aware of Preschoolers

As you walk about in the church or visit in a home be aware of preschoolers. Be available to them and become the friend of as many as will let you. Be conscious of opportunities to challenge their curiosity by calling attention to the feel and smell of the flower you are wearing or listening to the sound of your watch.

### Be "Huggable"

You are a figure of authority to preschoolers, and many may be afraid of you at first. But as you open your life to them they will love you for the warm, gentle person they are able to experience you as being. One of the greatest treats for them and you is that you allow them to hug you and feel your embrace in return.

## PARENTING PRESCHOOLERS

The preschool years are tremendously important to a person's emotional and spiritual development. Children are growing and learning at a rapid rate; parents are adjusting to parenthood and other adult responsibilities and the manner in which these issues are handled will influence later development.

Concepts and feelings about self, God, and others begin to be formulated very early in a child's life. Therefore, early experiences with a caring and accepting nurturer are of great importance. The child that has a sense of attunement with its nurturer has a major ingredient needed for good emotional and spiritual development.

There are three major issues that need to be considered by parents of young children. The first need of the child is to feel unconditionally loved and accepted. This issue needs to be addressed by parents before the child's birth, as well as the months immediately following. Both the mother and father need to honestly deal with the conditions they may secretly put on their unborn child and come to terms with them. For example, the gender of the child has already been determined at conception. So have all the other genetic characteristics of the child's life. Mother and father need to come to a place where they can joyfully receive the child as a gift from God. This major step indicates the emotional maturity parents need to raise an emotionally and spiritually healthy child.

Children who do not experience this type of acceptance will struggle with feelings of low self-esteem and a sense of unworthiness of their parents' love. The lack of unconditional acceptance can set a pattern of years of disappointing relationships as children act out the feelings that they, in some way, have been a disappointment to the most important people in their lives.

A second major issue is that of trust. Life with people and, ultimately, a positive relationship with God are conditioned by the child's ability to trust. How does a child learn to trust? How does a home environment that teaches distrust hinder the child's development?

Children learn trust as their needs are met consistently and lovingly. Babies are totally dependent on their parents for food and other basic care. If these needs are met lovingly children will learn that they are loved and that those caring for them can be trusted. Such things as holding the child, focused attention, playing with and enjoying the child, and talking with the child, build positive feelings in the parent-child relationship.

Children who do not have their needs met in a loving manner will feel rejected and will not develop the sense of trust they need. This distrust, or lack of trust, will make functioning in the world very difficult. The learned distrust or lack of trust will also make the idea of trusting God a rather formidable task. How can children believe that God is good and caring when they have experienced their parents as being untrustworthy?

The third major issue is that of becoming an individual apart from parents. The child's early life is so dependent upon the care of the parents, especially the mother, that becoming a separate person can be a significant struggle. When a child turns one, he or she has already been making progress toward some independence. As walking begins, physical and mental abilities continue to develop rapidly, and the child wants to and is increasingly able to do many things for himself or herself.

At this point, parents need to recognize the child's growing independence and adjust to this emerging individual. Balance is an important key for parents regarding the issue. The child is obviously not able to decide about what is safe or good in all instances. The parents' role is to allow and encourage independence where the child can handle it and give help as it is needed. Helping the child balance independence and dependence needs is an important step for parents and child. If parents and child negotiate this time well the child will be on his or her way to self-respect. From this sense of self grows a sense of personal responsibility and decision making that are a part of later development.

One final word needs to be said about the roles of mother and father during these foundational years. Both have highly significant roles in the child's development.

It is likely that most of the care in the child's early life will be given by the mother. She will set the emotional tone in which the child will be nurtured emotionally and spiritually. She will not be, and should not be expected to be, a perfect mother. However, if she wants the child, accepts the child, and lovingly meets the child's basic needs she will help her child make tremendous strides in emotional and spiritual growth.

But what about the role of the father? What is he to do regarding his child's development? Hopefully, he will assist as much as possible with meeting the child's basic needs. If there are other children he will want to assume as much of their care as possible. He needs to make himself available to do whatever he can to assure his wife of his support and care during this time. His basic role is to give his support to her so she can concentrate on providing the physical and emotional needs of the young child. He provides a loving, secure environment for his wife so that she can provide the same for their child.

## NOTES

1. From the *New American Standard.Bible.* Copyright The Lockman Foundation, 1960, 1962, 1963, 1968, 1971, 1972, 1973, 1975, 1977.

2. C. Sybil Waldrop, *Understanding Today's Preschoolers.* Nashville: Convention Press, 1982, p. 48.

3. Erik Erikson, *Identity, Youth, and Crisis.* New York: W.W. Norton & Co., Inc., 1968, pp. 96-107.

## ANNOTATED BIBLIOGRAPHY

Benson, Peter L., Judy Galbraith, and Pamela Espeland. *What Kids Need to Succeed*. Minneapolis: Free Spirit Publishing, Inc., 1995.

This book is about the kinds of developmental assets kids need to succeed in today's world. These assets are identified from a survey of over a quarter million young people in six hundred communities. The authors give numerous suggestions on how to build success-oriented assets in children at home, in the community, and in the congregation.

Lester, Andrew D. *Pastoral Care with Children in Crisis*. Philadelphia: The Westminster Press, 1985.

In this book Andrew Lester addresses two main issues. First, he deals with the fact that children are often in crisis and need a pastor to care for them. He shares insights into what children need from a pastor and basic principles of pastoral care with children. The second major area Lester approaches is methods of pastoral care with children. Here he gives some basic and helpful insights into the use of play, art, storytelling, and writing in the pastoral care of children.

Lester, Andrew W., Editor. *When Children Suffer*. Philadelphia: The Westminster Press, 1987.

This book is a compilation of the works of several writers on how to minister to children when they suffer from various types of issues. Part one focuses on some developmental understanding of children as a background for ministry. Part two deals with specific issues such as divorce, death, hospitalization, abuse, etc.

Scharff, David E. and Jill Savege Scharff. *Object Relations Family Therapy*. Northvale, NJ: Aronson, 1991.

This book is intended for persons interested in using the concept of object relations in family therapy. However, several chapters, particularly Chapter 3, can increase the reader's understanding of the importance of the early years in forming the child's perception of him or herself. Chapter 3 has a particularly good discussion of the roles of the mother and the father in raising a healthy child.

Chapter 2

# The Early School Years:
# Finding Acceptance Beyond the Family

Bruce P. Powers
Bruce Powers Jr.

Most ministers take for granted religious development in children. Consider congregations you know. Pastors typically spend about 90 percent of their time on worship, education, counseling, and administration concerns that focus primarily on adults. Very little time is devoted to direct involvement with children, and to activities that will assist parents as they influence the religious development of their children.

The problem with this is that the greatest potential for influencing Christian development is not with adolescents or adults, but with children and preschoolers. With preschoolers it is the loving, Christian nurture that has the greatest impact. With children it is the living example of their primary caregivers and the direct religious instruction (which gives guidance about beliefs and practices) that have the greatest influence.

The role of the minister in caring for children is basically relational: (1) how to relate to children, and (2) how to help parents relate to their children. Only when a minister is actively involved in both of these areas is a holistic concept of care for children being practiced.[1]

## FOCUS ON AGES SIX THROUGH TWELVE

This chapter deals specifically with the early school years, grades one through six (roughly ages six through twelve). It is written to assist ministers and other interested persons in dealing directly with the needs and concerns of children to foster their spiritual, emotional, and intellectual development.

The first part describes the growth of these children; gives characteristics of their spiritual, emotional, and intellectual development; and illustrates symptoms calling for an informed response by ministers, teachers, parents, and other caring persons. The latter portion focuses on providing appropriate spiritual nurture and suggestions for working with children, both directly and through the parents.

As you saw in the previous chapter, the initial impressions gained during preschool years are major imprints for subsequent phases of development. Growth occurs as a child successfully integrates and transforms the various facets of his or her life based on previous imprints and current reality. The information that follows builds on the premise that a child is capable, both physically and mentally, of achieving the transformations usually expected between ages six and twelve. Differences among children is normal, so symptoms and interventions regarding a wide range of behavior are presented. This information, however, is not necessarily applicable to those with obvious physical and psychological problems. In such cases, consult with or refer parents to a medical doctor or a child psychologist.

## HOW A CHILD DEVELOPS

Parents will often ask a minister or friend, "Is my child normal?" They look at other children of comparable age and wonder why their child is different. Some children walk, talk, etc., sooner than others. Many parents wonder if their child is "on schedule." Rather than addressing the issue of normality, it is more constructive to discuss what we can expect from developing children.

The school age years are marked by a great capacity for absorbing facts and for using information to solve problems. Children also develop skills in using their knowledge as they solve arithmetic problems, tell time, select clothes to wear, write letters, and some even master technology that many adults cannot understand. (Look at the children who can use a computer!)

As middle childhood approaches, children develop the ability to consider more than one factor at a time. This change leads to more flexible problem solving as well as the ability to make comparisons.

Along with intellectual development, there is steady growth of the body and ability to control it. Growth seems to come in spurts, and during the latter half of this age range, girls surpass boys in physical development.

Younger children must be active; they get restless when their bodies must be still. By middle childhood, however, they begin to develop the use of smaller muscles and the concentration that allows for longer periods of intense work and play. Physical skills, coordination, and endurance are the major developments by late childhood.

Emotionally, the child's major adjustment is identifying the authorities in his or her life. During preschool years, those who counted were the parents, or caregivers. Upon moving into the larger world of school and community, a child must sort out those persons and things that really count. Because they think and learn in a literal, concrete manner, children seek to identify the people and places that give the answers or tell the rules.

They then attempt to gain approval or get attention by following or imitating their authorities. For most children, those persons and things that have the greatest exposure or the respect of family and friends will most likely be viewed as authoritative. During the latter years of childhood, peers become more and more influential, gradually assuming a role of major authority during adolescence.

Socially, children must learn to interact appropriately with peers and develop a positive self-image. As the ability to make comparisons develops, there is the possibility that a child may feel inferior due to an inability to perform like other children. During late childhood, the social interests of boys and girls begin to diverge widely as they begin to gather in cliques and boys focus on boy-things and girls focus on girl-things.

## CHANGES FROM AGES SIX THROUGH TWELVE

Let us take this general overview and see how it plays out in the life of a typical child. Look for similarities in the children you know. The focus will be on intellectual development, which determines how a child processes experience and serves as the foundation for all other domains of development.

Jason is our typical child. Prior to entering first grade, his mental work consisted primarily of making relationships between experience and action. For example, he learned the connection between asking for a glass of milk and receiving it, bad behavior and punishment, hunger and eating, and the rules about day and night, hot and cold, happy and sad. Jason learned basic stimulus-response connections that are not created or thought out. He simply recognized the relationship between situations and actions according to the classical and operant conditioning previously experienced.

Around the sixth year, Jason began to make multiple connections. That is, he gradually gained the capacity to manipulate or rework information. This information was organized into unique patterns that become important to the child; and the child developed the ability to draw selectively from the material to answer questions and solve problems. Thus before age six, Jason wanted all of his toys; he did not like the idea of sharing if he wanted an item. Now he is learning that sharing can create friends, and that if he shares others will share with him. Assimilation of the information gained from these social interactions is an important task during these early school years.

Of all the intellectual and social developments during this age, the most important of these is reading. Learning to read is a natural act for most children, but does not come to all at the same time. In most cases, a child has a eureka moment when there is recognition of a written word. This insight cannot be forced on a child, but can be encouraged by exposure to the many different aids that teachers use to help children find the key, such as letter and picture flash cards.

Children learn to read by stringing the sounds of letters together. The eureka moment comes when a child sounds out all the letters in a word and realizes that it is the same word that he or she already uses in conversation. For one of our children, the word was *cab*. He saw a taxi stopped at a light and made the sounds, *kuh—a—buh*. He said it again slowly, then shouted, "*Cab!* That's a *cab!*"

The early childhood years are a time of rapid growth in cognitive ability. Jason is able to learn facts and information at an astounding rate through rote memorization. He has become an authority on many topics, looking for any opportunity to put his knowledge to use.

Attention span increases so that Jason is now interested in a continuing story from day to day, whereas previously everything was done in single episodes. Work, reading, and play sessions become longer, and there is an obvious effort to continue or get back to uncompleted tasks that were enjoyable.

During middle childhood, ages eight to ten, the greatest growth is in reading. The ability to translate symbols into sounds is a marvelous achievement that allows Jason to roam the world of adventure through the written word. Jason is also very interested in rules. He knows reasons for everything, can tell you why he is right and you are wrong, and will argue over the rules of a game he is playing as much as he will play the game.

During middle childhood a reading explosion occurs. Parents will watch with awe as children read dozens of books. In some cases, parents take this as a clue that the child is gifted and they begin to arrange special educational opportunities. In other cases, parents try to redirect the child's interest to more active pursuits such as recreation, household chores, and even homework. This heightened interest in reading is perfectly normal. Let Jason enjoy the new expanded world that reading provides.

In most instances, this extensive reading is not giftedness and is not an escape from responsibility; it is simply the right expression for the child's phase of development. There will be a gradual decline in reading time, so that by age thirteen, Jason will have to be encouraged to read and spend less time listening to music or talking on the phone.

Jason's imagination develops rapidly during middle childhood, enriching the adventures he has through reading. He actually is the space pilot, the detective, the mom or dad he is imitating. Make-believe becomes a very real game, and he wants you to act with him as if he were that person. Play characters soon give way, however, to acting out adventures. For boys, this is typically action-oriented (e.g., exploring and space fighters).

For girls, it can be action and activities such as homemaking or acting like a television personality. Both genders identify heroes, both real and fictional, whom they imitate.

Don't worry about the child's trips of fantasy. They are enjoyable experiences that allow the real to interact with the larger world that the child is coming to know. As intellectual growth continues, the real world wins, and children gradually lose the beautiful capacity to transcend the ordinary. One caution, however: If Jason increasingly lives in imaginary experiences and does not appear able to separate the real and the unreal, consult a physician for advice. By age twelve, a child should spend most of his or her time in the real world.

As Jason becomes an older child, his intelligence approaches maturity. His rote memory and arithmetical reasoning are almost at their peak; as he grows older, he will simply enrich and build on the basic skills acquired during this period.

By the end of this phase, he will have learned a massive amount of information, such as the multiplication tables, names of the states and their capitals, the names and categories of living things, and basic Christian beliefs.

Rote memory and logical thinking are major strengths of older children, but this does not mean that the child can do abstract and philosophical reasoning like an adult; these are the mental operations that are developing during this phase. Jason learns to ask and pose answers to *what if?* questions; he poses alternatives and considers options. He develops a little bit of the adult's suspicion, and becomes aware that everything is not exactly as it appears. For example, slight-of-hand magic can enthrall younger children; but the older child begins to look for the trick.

At the beginning of this phase, Jason would reason: After a rain, the grass is wet. The grass is wet this morning; therefore it rained. By the end, he would observe the wet grass and think: *Did it rain? Or did Dad turn on the sprinkler? Or is that dew on the front lawn?* Mental operations that were originally limited to the concrete, *I-see-it-therefore-it-is*, type of thinking enlarge to include abstract, or conjecture thinking (that is, when you consider possibilities).

Middle childhood is also the time for the flowering of artistic and athletic talent. Such expressions are not polished, mind you, but they are observable and can be encouraged through group and individual lessons.

During the late stages of childhood, these special aptitudes can emerge in remarkable ways. Adults need to be alert to special interests of children so as to cultivate their development whenever possible. But be careful not to impose adult or parental ambitions; children must develop what God has given *them*.

During the two years prior to adolescence, Jason has experienced a slowing down of the rapid growth he had earlier. This creates some problems, since girls continue to grow during this time and for a year or two, surpass boys of the same age.

Children are able to learn complex motor skills, and often will devote a great deal of time to developing both individual and team skills. With this development, the competitive spirit becomes a major influence on a child's activity. These physical developments blend with the emotional changes that occur prior to adolescence.

There is great variety among the activities of older children as each seeks to find others who have similar interests and compatible needs. Feeling good about oneself, achieving a sense of independence, and acceptance among peers are the focal concerns, and obviously are interrelated. This can lead to a few close playmates, who may view themselves as a special group or club.

Competition is handled by seeking those who are like or who will accept you; thus there are three general patterns that help children cope with this need: a close-knit group of boys, a close-knit group of girls, and the loner. Loners cannot find others with similar interests and needs, or do not find fulfillment in competing with others. Children who continue to lose themselves in reading or other indoor activity instead of group play, are in this category.

Childhood ends with a blend of adventure, competition, physical well-being, and a strong sense of self-reliance. The child during these years has dealt with three major spheres of development:

- Integration of the rather limited experiences of family and home with the larger sphere of peer and community influences.
- Development of logical processes that enable a person to move from concrete to abstract thinking—to function in the realm of adult concepts and communication.
- Development of physical skills that allow one to compete in individual and team activities.

## THE CHILD AND SPIRITUALITY

The ways in which a child develops religious concepts can be inferred from the information given above, but for reference, the following is a nutshell summary.

Prior to age six, a child's religious concepts are primarily intuitive, and come from participation in and observation of the faith experiences of his or her caregivers. During childhood years, there is a gradual move to take part in and adopt for oneself the stories, beliefs, and practices that are a part of the child's family and church.

These religious concepts are absorbed through informal exposure as well as through intentional, structured experiences. Learning focuses on literal interpretations, with distinct rules for judging right and wrong, good and bad. Authority is very important, and conformity—doing things like they are supposed to be done—is a virtue. Peer pressure is not as much an issue for the child as it is for the adolescent.

At the beginning of this phase, the child must learn to be a participant—that is, learn how to be accepted and feel secure. By ten or eleven, the child will have developed authoritative rules, reasons, and answers to categorize his or her faith. In many ways, these concepts are a composite of the informal and formal religious impressions that the child has assimilated and codified. Literal interpretations of the Bible and any other authority source such as a book, television program, preacher, teacher, or police officer are to be expected during this age.

Approaching puberty, faith concepts of peers become increasingly important; the molding influence of significant persons and groups with whom the child-youth identifies begins to substitute for the authorities accepted earlier. This peer orientation usually becomes evident at about twelve, and can be a dominant influence throughout life.

At this point, children pattern their lives according to the norms expressed by those who are important to and accepting of them. Beliefs and practices may be highly consistent with those experienced earlier, or they may represent a radical departure, depending on the significant others one chooses.[2]

## TASKS TO BE ACCOMPLISHED

You now have the basic developmental pattern that might be expected in children. To summarize, it would be helpful to recall the developmental tasks associated with childhood. You may remember that the necessity of achieving certain tasks during each age period was first proposed by Robert Havighurst.[3]

These tasks grow out of the three spheres of development mentioned earlier. They represent the achievements needed to enable persons to adjust successfully at their current age and prepare them to progress satisfactorily into the next phase of life.

Although these tasks have been enlarged and interpreted in a variety of ways, the basic need for children to achieve certain competencies as proposed by Havighurst remains. A knowledge of these is needed to assess the developmental issues operating in the life of a child as well as diagnosing areas of deficiency in those entering puberty.

For your information and reference, they are listed in Figure 2.1.

## *Practical Dimensions*

Let us turn now to the spiritual nurture of children and the practical information and guidelines that can be shared with parents and used by church ministers. In caring for persons, there is no substitute for the quality of living and relationship that you share with those you are seeking to serve. This is true for all ages, but especially so for children; they are so indelibly influenced by example and by the treatment they receive from authority figures.

FIGURE 2.1. Tasks to Be Accomplished During Childhood

To adjust successfully and to prepare for the next phase of life, a child entering puberty should have accomplished the following at a level appropriate for the society in which he or she lives.

1. Physical skills necessary for ordinary games.
2. Wholesome attitudes toward oneself as a growing person.
3. Ability to get along with age-mates.
4. Appropriate masculine or feminine role identification.
5. Fundamental skills in reading, writing, and calculating.
6. Concepts and abstract thinking necessary for everyday living.
7. Conscience, morality, and a scale of values.
8. Personal independence.
9. Attitudes to facilitate social interaction in groups and within institutions.

*Source:* Adapted from Havighurst, 1972, pp. 19-35.

What you do most of the time will have to come from a sense of rightness—giving and receiving, initiating, and responding—based on the felt needs of any situation. This you must learn to do without developing a game plan based on formalized theories and techniques. This is the informed minister, caring for persons out of who and what you are.

However, there are times when specific information and strategies are required in order to develop your personal skills, or to improve the total care provided within the life of a family, an age group in a church, or within a total congregation. Such information and actions are termed *interventions*—those preventive or prescriptive steps taken by a caregiver to direct or redirect the development of others in order to solve a real or potential problem.

The remainder of this chapter focuses on information and actions that can be used in both preventive and prescriptive ways with children and their parents. The material is not designed so much as a sequential teaching device as it is a reference section. As such, you can read it straight through, or you can simply turn to one of the topical headings for some concise information and/or guidelines.

The information may be directed toward ministers, but also relates directly to parents and other caring persons in a congregation. Each section is easily adaptable for use in relating to the age group or in assisting others in improving their caregiving.


## A CHILD'S POSITION IN THE FAMILY

The information provided thus far is for children in general. Some will develop exactly as described; others will vary widely, even in the same family. Of special significance, according to many authorities, are the changes that occur when there are two or more children in a family. Although there are many related influences that might produce similar responses—gender of a child, role models, peers, and stability of home life—the one predictable influence that is at the root of a great many pastoral care issues is a child's position among siblings.

Rudolf Dreikus and Loren Grey are two of the specialists who have provided helpful guidance on this topic. For many years they have been seeking to alert professionals to the major impact position in the family has on a child's development. Their book, *A Parents' Guide to Child Discipline*, was a central resource for preparing this section.[4]

### The Oldest Child

The first child is the major attraction and thrives on being the central figure in the newly developed family triad. Being first and only (except in the case of multiple births, of course), the first child develops just as described earlier, until a brother or sister is born. Child number one is displaced, at least temporarily, and can experience this as rejection. Having had all the attention, he or she now has to seek a share of the parents' time.

If the age difference between the siblings is three years or less, this cannot be explained to the older child. He or she must be given extra attention in order to keep from feeling rejected; if this is not done, the child will seek attention in whatever way possible. Often, the older child will compete for attention by regressing to babyhood. Regression takes the form of babylike behaviors such as lapses in toilet training, demanding to be held or carried, thumbsucking, and so on.

While these behaviors can be distressing, they are normal and will disappear with time and attention. Even up to age five, the shock is rather extreme. But for the older child, an explanation is helpful. They can be lovingly guided into the joy of becoming one of the caregivers for the newborn.

You will notice that, as a group, firstborn children tend to be more conservative, to prefer authority—they like to give orders— and tend to dislike change. Since parents probably gave them more responsibility in early years, they tend to be better administrators and managers than those who were second and third children.

### The Second Child

Although the first child is displaced as the single recipient of parental affection, the second child comes to view the situation differently. He or she sees the older sibling as the pacesetter, as number one in terms of ability and in the attention received from parents. Consequently, the basic imprint for the second child is to equal, and even pass, the older child. If frustrated, the child will turn to behavior and/or pursuits that gain attention, usually either regressive and antisocial actions or activities in which the child can excel.

Research suggests that second children are usually much more flexible than first children, and see change as a means of gaining power. They are more likely to be creative, but are less consistent than first children in carrying out their ideas.[5]

### The Middle Child

If a third child arrives, displacement must be added to the adjustment problems already faced by the second child. According to Dreikus and Grey, a middle child usually discovers that it is necessary not only to compete in one area with a sibling who is larger and stronger and more capable, but must share his or her attention and affection with the new arrival.[6]

An obvious tension develops in middle children as they are seeking acceptance and affirmation. They feel pulled between being like the older sibling and being like the newborn. This becomes a basic question of identity, an issue that a middle child will often carry throughout life unless resolved early.

The basic need for a middle child, then, is affirmation as an individual. Equal time and caring from parents, not from an older sibling or other substitute, will help the child to resolve the identity crisis he or she feels.

### The Youngest Child

The youngest child in a family has a unique advantage related to attention and parental affection. He or she is never displaced by a younger sibling. Although there may be extremes of behavior to secure additional attention, the youngest child never has to surrender the tolerance and laxity of parental demands accorded to the baby in a family.

Consequently, this is the child often viewed as being spoiled, the one who needs to have his or her way, the one who needs to be cared for. In the extreme, this person gradually becomes overly dependent on others—a leaner in adulthood—or a manipulator, who seeks to get his or her needs met without considering the impact on others.

Perhaps due to the great ambiguity perceived by the youngest child in the values and practices within his or her family, this child grows up trying to make sense of a myriad of social, emotional, and intellectual stimuli coming from mother, father, and all the sibling parent figures. The youngest is the most likely child to break with the patterns of belief and practice held by the parents. An example of this is the child who chooses an occupation or follows a style of living in which the personality characteristics or activities run counter to the prevailing family pattern.[7]

### The Only Child

This child is never displaced, but never has one close in age or capability with whom to interact. Therefore, the only child must orient himself or herself entirely to the parents. The only child may display some of the characteristics of the youngest child, but this seems to be influenced largely by how the parents treat the child—most often seen are the only children who are raised and cared for as babies regardless of age, and those who are brought up as little adults.

Although it usually takes the only child longer to develop the skills to relate socially with peers, Dreikus and Grey do not think this significantly affects a person's ability to adjust to the world as an adult.[8]

## THE FAMILY AS A SYSTEM

It is easy to see that the family is not just a collection of individuals, and that it is not simply a composite of its members. Rather it is, as often referred to in family counseling literature and workshops, a system. There are no simple answers and no pat interventions that will guarantee success for parents, teachers, and others who work with the family. The reason is this: *whatever happens in any part of the interrelated family system ultimately influences and is influenced by every other part.*

The best we can do, therefore, is to seek the best understanding possible, and to develop consistent practices based on principles and guidelines that are consistent with Christian ideals and personal conscience.

This material assumes some awareness of the family as a system. The developmental issues that have been presented, as well as the practical suggestions that follow, require that they be viewed from a holistic perspective. To treat one action or one event in pastoral care without getting in touch with the larger context is like a physician treating a symptom rather than seeking the cause of the symptom.[9]

In terms of dealing with children, it is important to keep in mind that a "problem" child functions as part of the family system. View a particular child's behavior, therefore, as a symptom rather than a cause.

As you seek to be a caregiver, your need is threefold:

- Be informed about the developmental needs of children.
- Provide care and counsel with an awareness of the larger system within which the child lives.
- Know your limitations; refer cases to appropriate child and family care specialists when you are unsure of or unable to provide the care required.

## REWARD AND PUNISHMENT

Why do kids do what they do? Behavior is shaped by its consequences, that is by the reward and/or punishment received. If you would like to see more of certain behaviors, you have to reward the child for engaging in those actions. If, however, you would like to see less of a certain behavior, you can do one or both of the following things:

- Punish the child when the undesired behavior is exhibited.
- Remove the rewards that have served to maintain the undesired behavior.

Remember, though, that no two people are exactly alike in what they seek: one child's punishment may be another's reward. So be alert for individual differences.[10]

In providing punishment for misbehavior, be aware that the child's actions may be a ploy to get attention or to gain status. An unknowing adult may very well fall for a child's unconscious scheme, and reinforce the undesired behavior.

Although you intend to punish a child, the fact that the child gets attention or gets you into a struggle for power may give the child the very reward desired—the child wins by getting you into the struggle. Consequently, social separation and isolation handled by an adult in a calm manner is often a good strategy for punishment.[11]

## *RULES*

The following are basic guidelines to use in developing and using rules, whether for home or for church:

1. Provide structure and security by establishing reasonable and clear rules appropriate for the child's age and ability.
2. Make rules short and state positively if possible.
3. Be clear about the consequences if rules are not followed.
4. Ask children to help make up some of the rules.
5. Where rules are not necessary, give specific boundaries within which the child must function.
6. As age and dependability increase, broaden the boundaries, renegotiate the rules, and involve the child in making decisions.
7. Be firm, consistent, and fair in the application of rules.

## *CHILDHOOD STRESS*

Of immediate concern to counselors is what child psychologists now are identifying as childhood stress. This condition, they suggest, ultimately affects one's perspective and emotional/physical well-being as an adult. David Elkind, author of *The Hurried Child*, says that the children of the previous generation can be characterized as those with too little discipline. But those of this decade are the *hurried* children. They are forced to achieve more, earlier, than any other generation. The result of this pressure to achieve, to succeed, to please, is a disease in which "children are stressed by the fear of failure—of not achieving fast enough or high enough."[12]

Whereas major emphasis in childhood used to be on recreation in a general sense (such as swimming, hiking, pick-up ball games, and make-believe adventures) the focus now is on specialized training (such as foreign languages, travel, tennis, soccer, dance, and computers). The most popular of these current activities seems to be those that specialize in competition, where there is a strong desire to teach the finer points, participate in rigorous skill development, and perform in the likeness of adults.

This push in our society also allows children to become status symbols for their parents, teachers, and others who coach them. For example, the push and pride often associated in the past with colleges and prep schools now extends to private preschools, kindergartens, and special elementary school programs. In all of this is the pressure to get children on the right track early.[13]

Where do you see this in your community? Look for a push on intellectual attainment, such as a gifted and talented program at the kindergarten level. What about the push for physical achievement? Is the level of competition and intensive coaching extending to the preschool years? How are the children dressing? Are they picking up on designer clothes and styled hair?

Elkind points out that up to about age eight, this pressure can be perceived by the child as rejection. After that, they seem to welcome the rapid advance toward adult-oriented achievement. The result is selective maturity in the child, with a disjointed sense of wholeness (both as they see it and as we see it). We can mistake this rapid advance in one or two areas as real maturity, rather than seeing it simply as a game we and they are playing.[14]

The cure must come from parents, from teachers, from society. Without a change, the qualities that come from five or six years of being a child—playfulness, creativity, adventure, learning to be independent—can be lost in a pressure-packed life that focuses always on bigger and better. In David Elkind's words, "It is children's right to be children, to enjoy the pleasures, and to suffer the pains . . ."[15]

## CHILDREN AND CRISIS

Despite the pressures of growing up, this period is perhaps the least stressful in all of life. The child is mobile, has a degree of independence, is adventuresome, is greatly resilient, is at the healthiest point in life, and thinks there is an answer and an easy fix-it for everything.

Crises such as divorce, a family move, death of a loved one, or major illness do cause disruption, but usually there is great capacity for accepting and moving on with the realities of life. Whereas many adults will be very slow to deal with the stress of acceptance and reintegration involved in resolving crisis situations, children usually will express themselves openly, and very quickly begin to reconstruct their world in light of new situations.

Adults often struggle to look at all the reasons, and to explain what should or should not happen; they review many alternatives and search for more; many times they become overwhelmed, and consequently depressed, due to the hopelessness they perceive. Children, however, deal with crisis situations much more *concretely;* even their *what if?* questions usually deal with practical matters (e.g., "What if grandpa does not get well; who will take me fishing?"). Children in crisis usually are not ministered to alone; rather they are cared for as part of a family grouping. This point is important since caregiving in such situations is often directed toward the adults or the family group.

Rarely does a child receive his or her share of needed, *individual* attention. Perhaps simply calling this to your attention will be encouragement enough to focus more attention directly on the child.

What should be done? The child needs to tell his or her story without being judged. There is a need for emotional and perhaps even physical contact that will be accepting and supportive. Simple statements that reflect the child's expressions may help to convey understanding and acceptance: "You miss grandpa"; "You loved him very much"; "He loved you very much"; "It is hard to believe that he is no longer with us."

Responding with short, simple expressions and, if requested, facts given simply and honestly, will reassure the child. If accompanied by an affectionate hug and a loving look, the child will be able to face the situation with an added sense of personal worth and security.[16]

Fear and anxiety are a normal part of crisis, and usually are short term. However, if these appear excessive or continue to be expressed after the crisis has been resolved, referral of the parents and child to a specialist is advisable.

Concerning a child's terminal illness, the same principles described above apply. Again, care must be provided in the context of the family system. Many times you will find that the child will be more accepting of the situation than will the parents.

## SUGGESTIONS TO SHARE WITH PARENTS

Here are some rather pointed suggestions that can be shared with parents or adapted for a minister's relations with children in the congregation.

Remember, the phases of childhood development described in this chapter, while occurring about the ages given, are not a rule. There are wide differences among children, even in the same family. Be aware that you can help and encourage, but that you develop for the child. With that caution, here are some ideas to share with parents:

1. Be alert to special interests and expressions from your child and seek to cultivate these whenever possible. But be careful not to impose parental ambitions on your child; he or she must develop what God has given him or her.

2. Listen, observe, and talk with your child about schoolwork and home activities. Watch for persistent problems such as the reversing of letters as in the words *saw* and *was*. Discuss your observations with school and church teachers to see if you need to seek consultation with a physician or education specialist.

3. A child's self-esteem is very important. Don't belittle a child who is not progressing as fast as another. Encourage and love each child at the level on which he or she is operating. So much of a child's development happens at a point of readiness; be patient.

4. Avoid using adult logic and abstract concepts to explain why a child should or should not do something. It is beneficial to discuss rules and why they must be followed on a level the child can understand. Do not, however, try to explain why a child should follow directions. A simple, "Because I asked you to" is fine.

5. Read and write with your children. Go to the library with them. Read to younger children; then let them tell you the story while pointing to the pictures. Listen to older children read; talk about their response. Encourage creative writing and the writing of letters. Younger children can dictate as you write. Tell short stories to each other.

6. Encourage memory work and reward significant achievement with a homemade certificate or a special surprise. Be patient and listen to all of the rote material; assist when possible. Please note that a big difference exists between encouraging performance with the promise of rewards and simply rewarding or praising a job well done. If children are taught to work for rewards, the behavior disappears as soon as the rewards stop coming.

7. Discuss life experiences together. Talk about movies you see, stories you read together, things that happen at church and in the community. Talk about how you feel about Jesus, church, friends, and your home. Focus on feelings and things you and the child do. Ask for your child's opinions on things. This will create many wonderful opportunities for informal learning.

8. Be selective in television viewing. Don't let television be the major influence in your child's home environment. Be sure to discuss and process what your child sees to counteract the negative values that television often teaches.

9. Evaluate the influences in your home. Take a tour. Look at the pictures, the reading material, the arrangement of furniture, the games. Then consider the influence that parents, older brothers and sisters, and neighbors have. Determine the specific things you want to do to influence and nurture your child's development.

## DEVELOPING SPIRITUALITY

The role of leaders and parents is not to make spiritual children. Their faith is a gift from God, that comes as they embrace the *One* and the *ones* who love them. For children, Christian nurture is the most important influence on the extent and quality of their spirituality. The objective for leaders and parents is to develop a Christ-centered and Bible-based environment for children, thereby giving them the best opportunity to respond by imitating God, as God's beloved children (see Ephesians 5:1-4).

The following are specific ways to develop caring and supportive relationships with children, their parents, and volunteer leaders who work with the children. These actions by themselves, however, will not make spiritual children. The significant people in a child's life must live and love as God's beloved children. Children will learn to imitate God by imitating their primary caregivers. The essence of passing on faith is to tell *and* live the gospel story, and allow God to work in the lives of all.

Whether you are a minister serving on a large church staff, the pastor of a small church, or serve in related positions, these ideas can be adapted to your particular situation and ministry style. Read these over, perhaps adding some ideas of your own; then consider ways to enrich your ministry with children.

1. Make it known that you are a minister to children as well as to adults. Communicate this through the regular channels for church public relations as well as through your personal contact with children and parents. This does not have to be a publicity campaign; rather it should be an intentional effort to speak to the needs of children with the same frequency that you speak to the needs of adults or of youth.
2. Get acquainted with children as persons in their own right. For example, call them by their names, visit them in their Sunday school departments, occasionally attend one of their socials, or have children visit your home for a party.
3. Look at children as you would an adult. Be aware of your posture when speaking with them. When you are visiting with them individually or in small groups, try to maintain eye level.

4. When communicating use simple, direct language—no big words. Don't ask thought questions as you might use with adults; rather ask factual questions based on either the material being studied or on what you could expect a child to have experienced. Tell about things that can be seen, felt, or heard.

5. Give some of your teaching time to this age group. This can be done periodically through a children's sermon, in a Sunday school class, a church training group, in vacation Bible school, or through an inquirer's class for children considering a profession of faith.

6. Schedule a regular time to visit the children's departments in your church. Work with department leaders to find a convenient time. On some occasions you could teach or talk with the children about a prearranged topic. At other times you could perhaps be a helper and work at a table with the regular teacher and children.

7. Set up a visitation plan that will assure at least two personal, noncrisis visits to each child during ages six to twelve. These pastoral calls would be to visit the child so that you can get acquainted, learn names, and develop/improve your relationship with each other. One of the best plans is to visit each child as he or she turns eight years old (they will have a desire to know you and will be intrigued by your work by this age). Then, in another planned visit as each child turns eleven, you could explore the child's understanding of and readiness to consider steps toward a profession of faith.

8. In your formal responsibilities, such as in a worship service, draw from the world of the child for some of your illustrations, refer occasionally to some of the lessons and songs children are using in Sunday school, and periodically ask all ages to participate in an activity that children love and can do well. If you feel comfortable doing it, use a child from time to time in place of an adult, to perform a congregational activity like reading scripture, praying, or giving a report at a business meeting.

9. Conduct a periodic conference for parents. The emphasis might change from time to time, but the general focus should

be on family life, parenting, and religious education of children. Conduct some of these sessions yourself, and invite specialists in for others. Ask parents to help identify topics to be considered. Many churches are able to include these sessions during their regular training periods, using materials produced by denominational offices.

10. Provide crisis care for children just as you do for adults. They rejoice and they experience sorrow—just in a more concrete way than do older persons. They experience pressure, and they get depressed—but their high activity level usually helps them snap back faster than adults. When counseling them, ask them to name their feelings, or to tell you what the feelings look like. Be accepting; empathize with the child. Try to give assurance that he or she is loved and cared for. When praying, suggest that the child talk with God. If the child is hesitant, ask if you should take turns praying or if he or she would rather have you pray.

11. To help with faith development, tell and retell the great stories of the Church. Talk with children about the stories, and encourage them to tell the ones they like to hear.

12. Involve children in the mission and witness the church in the community. Whenever possible, let children participate in acts of Christian service and outreach along with older church members.

13. Provide opportunity for cross-generational learning and fellowship. Engage all ages on a regular basis in some meaningful activity. This is referred to in a number of ways, like extended family, intergenerational education, family clusters, and all-age learning. The idea is to break down barriers among the age groups.

14. Children tend to mark their religious growth by significant events. Determine the regular events (such as Easter, baptism, and homecoming) that are important to your congregation, and the personal events (such as birth of a brother or sister, moving, and starting back to school) that are important to children. Develop consistent ways to recognize and/or celebrate such occasions. These become the rituals that children refer to as they build their religious concepts in later years.

15. Be aware that the church is teaching its young through every activity, whether planned or unplanned. The structured teaching is but a small part; the influence of shared life is a major part. Examine with a critical eye the life and ministry of your church. The style of Christian living, the level of caring, and the quality of life together will be the overwhelming determinants on the religious convictions developed by those growing up in your congregation.

16. Look for chances to interact with children in informal settings. Spend some time hanging out with them, play the games they like to play. Informal, unstructured interactions can be a powerful ministry tool. The children will come to see you as a friend, they will feel special due to the attention, and you will have the opportunity to teach and be a role model simply by being with them.

## THE TRANSITION TO ADOLESCENCE

As children move into adolescence, look for them to shift from an authority-centered approach to life and religion to a peer-oriented society. Social values and spirituality that were defined by parents and teachers gradually become blended in a matrix of testing limits and searching for identity. The spirituality that was expressed in right behavior and rote answers during childhood, gradually becomes an important resource for the searching process.

As you will examine in the next chapter, the spiritual nurture and the biblical foundations gained during the childhood years can provide young people with support to search for their own answers to life. The foundations of childhood can provide a rich resource as young teens begin to make their own decisions.

## NOTES

1. The equipping role of the minister in assisting parents is an increasing concern in our society. See, for example, George Gallup Jr. and David Poling, *The Search for America's Faith.* Nashville: Abingdon, 1980, pp. 41-55.

2. The subject of faith development is crucial for Christians; it is at the root of our reason for being. To acquaint yourself more thoroughly with what is happen-

ing to persons and ways to be more effective in assisting them—and in nurturing your own faith development—see *Growing Faith*, by Bruce P. Powers. Nashville: Broadman Press, 1982.

3. See Robert J. Havighurst, *Developmental Tasks and Education*, Third Edition. New York: David McKay Co., 1972, pp. 19-35.

4. Rudolf Dreikus and Loren Grey, *A Parents' Guide to Child Discipline*. New York: Hawthorne Books, 1970, p. 12f.

5. Ibid., p. 14.

6. Ibid., p. 14.

7. Ibid., p. 14.

8. Ibid., p. 15.

9. An excellent resource on the systemic nature of pastoral care is E. Mansell Pattison, *Pastor and Parish—A Systems Approach*. Philadelphia: Fortress Press, 1977.

10. Dreikus and Grey, op. cit., p. 21.

11. Ibid., p. 17.

12. David Elkind, *The Hurried Child*. Reading, MA: Addison-Wesley, 1981, p. xii.

13. Ibid., p. 36f.

14. Ibid., p. 189.

15. Ibid., p. 200.

16. Haim G. Ginott, *Between Parent and Child*. New York: The Macmillan Company, 1965, pp. 145-146.

## ANNOTATED BIBLIOGRAPHY

Aleshire, Donald O. *Faith Care*. Philadelphia: The Westminster Press, 1988.

Covers spirituality issues with major emphasis on children and family.

Cully, Iris V. *Christian Child Development*. San Francisco: Harper and Row, 1979.

Gives basic background on what to expect as a child grows spiritually, emotionally, and physically.

Davis, Cos H. Jr. *Children and the Christian Faith*. Nashville: Broadman Press, 1979.

Overview of how to relate to children in the church and in the home.

Dreikus, Rudolf and Loren Grey. *A Parents' Guide to Child Discipline*. New York: Hawthorne Books, 1970.

A secular look at discipline.

Eimers, Robert and Robert Aitchison. *Effective Parents, Responsible Children*. New York: McGraw-Hill, 1977.

A secular look at responsible parenting.

Elkind, David. *The Hurried Child*. Reading, MA: Addison-Wesley, 1981.

Discusses pressures children experience and ways to resolve.

Gallup, George Jr. and David Poling. *The Search for America's Faith*. Nashville: Abingdon, 1980.

A review of the changes taking place in the home and society with relevance for developments leading into the twenty-first century.

Ginott, Haim G. *Between Parent and Child*. New York: The Macmillan Co., 1965.

A basic resource for parenting.

Havighurst, Robert J. *Developmental Tasks and Education*, Third Edition. New York: David McKay Co., 1972.

The original overview of Havighurst's well-known tasks.

Pattison, E. Mansell. *Pastor and Parish—A Systems Approach*. Philadelphia: Fortress Press, 1977.

An overview of systems theory and its relationship to congregational life.

Powers, Bruce P. *Growing Faith*. Nashville: Broadman Press, 1982.

A study of, and case studies that illustrate, the faith development process among Christians.

# Chapter 3

# Adolescence: Stuck in the Middle

## James L. Minton

Any effort to define adolescence precipitates several questions. Do you define adolescence based on when it starts? What is going on during that period? What happens as you emerge from adolescence into early adulthood? All three of these questions are valid in developing a definition.

Relative to when adolescence begins, many suggestions have been offered:

- The levels of adult hormones in the bloodstream rise sharply.
- Someone first thinks about dating.
- Girls are eleven years old; when boys are thirteen.
- An interest in the opposite sex begins.
- Children become unexpectedly moody.
- Children form exclusive social cliques.
- Children think about becoming emotionally independent of their parents.
- Children worry about the way their bodies look.
- Children enter seventh grade.
- Peers' opinions influence children more than the opinions of their parents.
- Children begin to wonder who they really are.[1]

There is a kernel of truth in each of these statements, yet none can stand alone as a definition of the beginning of adolescence.

Relative to events during the adolescent period, just use your imagination for a definition. Youth of the nineties and the coming new century will be bombarded from every direction by "environ-mental forces" that bend, stretch, challenge, question, and distort their senses of reality and worth. Two key words emerge to describe adolescent functioning in today's world: status and survival.

Clearer definitions of events may be stated for the young person who passes out of adolescence into young adulthood. Although no chronological age can be affixed, several things become evident accordingly to Robert J. Havighurst. The young person begins to, among other things:

- Select and prepare for an occupation.
- Develop intellectual skills and concepts necessary for civic competence.
- Achieve socially responsible behavior.
- Prepare for marriage and family life.
- Develop a value system as a guide to ethical behavior.[2]

## DEFINITIONS

With this material as a background, we now look at three differ-ent perspectives from which to view adolescence as we develop definitions for each perspective. The different perspectives may be stated simply as biological, social, and psychological.

Social scientists with a biological orientation might define adoles-cence as the time between the onset of puberty and the completion of bone growth. Social scientists with a psychological orientation might define adolescence in terms of how adolescents think and feel about themselves and their world. Theorists with a social orientation (psychologists or sociologists) might define adolescence in terms of their participation in larger society as neither children nor adults, but in between.

Biologically, adolescent behavior is explained in terms of the physical changes that take place in the adolescent. Psychologically, adolescent behavior is explained in terms of changes in thinking and feeling (personality development). Socially, adolescent behavior is explained as a response to a marginal status in society. Any attempt at a complete definition of adolescence would have to include all of these.

## THEORIES

Let us now move into the theories of adolescent development. These theories are generally placed into four categories: biological, sociological, psychoanalytical, and cognitive.

### Biological Theorists: G. Stanley Hall and Arnold Gesell

The first of the major biological theories of adolescence was formulated by G. Stanley Hall (1904, 1905). Hall was heavily influenced by the work of Charles Darwin and sought to apply the principles of evolution to an understanding of adolescent development.[3] Hall's contention was that in the course of their development, children would progress through a series of stages similar to those through which the race had progressed in its evolutionary history. Hall's "recapitulation theory" also suggested that the course of development was largely genetically predetermined. Therefore, he strongly urged parents not to be too upset with the way their offspring were acting in any particular stage because it would pass, just as our history did. Hall advocated that it would come and go regardless of the child's environment because the course of development was determined by genetics alone. Subsequent evidence of anthropological nature (not including obvious Christian beliefs)—demonstrating that children do indeed behave very differently in different cultures, and demonstrating as well that the environment does have a significant effect on a child's development—has largely invalidated this aspect of the theory.[4]

One aspect of Hall's theory has found limited contemporary support. He described adolescence as a time of "storm and stress." This was an expression borrowed from a literary movement of the time, and Hall thought that adolescence paralleled the movement's commitment to excessive idealism and rebelliousness against established order. Most theorists will agree that there are stormy and stressful times in the life of an adolescent. Some will go even further and suggest that these times are necessary and are the motivation force in developing a stable self-concept.

A second major biological theorist was Arnold Gesell. Like Hall, Gesell based his developmental theories on the belief that biological factors were largely responsible for the personality characteristics of children at various stages in their development. Unlike Hall, however, he gave the environment an important role in accounting for variations among individuals.[5]

Gesell's theory has been described as a maturational theory, a spiral growth theory, and an age-profile theory. His theory is called a maturational theory because of his strong belief that various capabilities, as well as personality characteristics, result from the genetically predetermined unfolding of a maturational sequence. It is called a spiral growth theory because it involves the individual making progress, followed by a regression, followed by even further progress. This regression or "fall back" time gives an individual time to consolidate the gains made in progression and better assimilate them. And finally, it is an age-profile theory because much of Gesell's work described the progress made by the adolescent at different age levels.

Gesell's age levels for adolescence began at ten and ended at sixteen. He was ahead of his time to start at ten years old, but he stopped several years short at sixteen. Gesell was aware of the weaknesses in such an approach as this, but he did provide a measuring stick for accomplishments and characteristics for the young person based on a chronological age.

The following is a short summary of Gesell's age levels. Please keep in mind that the descriptions of these ages was last revised in 1956.

- *Ten-year-old*—well-adjusted, highly sensitive to fairness, confident, obedient, and fond of home. He or she is careless in appearance and not interested in the opposite sex.
- *Eleven-year-old*—moody, restless, rebellious, and quarrelsome. He or she is given to long periods of silence and argues with both parents and siblings.
- *Twelve-year-old*—more reasonable and tolerant, more influenced by his or her peers, more independent of his or her parents, and becomes painfully aware of his or her appearance, and is for the first time showing interest in the opposite sex.
- *Thirteen-year-old*—sullen, withdrawn, and very sensitive to criticism. He or she is tense, critical, highly self-conscious,

and has fewer friends than a year ago, but the ones he or she does have are a lot closer.
- *Fourteen-year-old*—suddenly an extrovert. He or she is confident and outgoing, spends hours discussing personalities and characters with friends, and has frequent identifications with heroes.
- *Fifteen-year-old*—has a rising spirit of independence. He or she is boisterous, rebellious, unpredictable, and has increased tensions. Conflicts with parents and school personnel are on the rise. It doesn't seem like it, but fifteen is the beginning of self-control.
- *Sixteen-year-old*—is self-confident and has a more balanced and integrated personality. He or she is cheerful, friendly, outgoing, well-adjusted, shows very little rebelliousness, and is future-oriented—the prototype of the preadult.[6]

Gesell's theory has several weak points. Girls are usually one and one-half to two years ahead of boys in terms of biological changes at the beginning of adolescence. Chronological age is not the best index of social, emotional, and physical development during adolescence. And finally, these profiles do not take into consideration early and late maturers or the various effects of home, school, or peer groups.

## Sociological Theorist: Robert J. Havighurst

Havighurst is possibly the most well-known sociological theorist regarding adolescent development. In the early 1950s, he identified ten developmental tasks for the adolescent. The young person strives to accomplish these tasks as he or she progresses through the adolescent period. After twenty years, Havighurst revised his work and presented a set of eight tasks. The tasks represented the skills, knowledge, functions, and attitudes that young people acquired through physical maturation, social expectations, and personal effort. Mastery of adolescent tasks results in maturity. Failure to master the adolescent tasks results in anxiety, social disapproval, and possibly the inability to function as a mature person. A brief description of each of the eight tasks follows. Please keep in mind that there are differences in accomplishment, sequence, and priority for different socioeconomic classes of adolescents.[7]

- *Forming new and more mature relationships with age-mates of both sexes.* The adolescent must move from the same-sex interests and playmates of middle childhood to include hetero-sexual friendships—which is the forerunner for the male-female relationships of adulthood.
- *Achieving a masculine or feminine social role.* Certain behaviors, attitudes, and values are expected of men and women. Social forces are causing changes in what is expected of a man and what is expected of a woman. Unless adolescents accept their own sexuality as a male or female and find an acceptable sex role, they will feel and be maladjusted.
- *Accepting one's physique and using the body effectively.* Adolescents are often extreme in their concern over the physical developments of their own bodies. Some changes are happening too fast, while others are going too slow. Some adolescents are pleased with their bodies, but most can easily find faults. Most adolescents wonder if they are "normal."
- *Achieving emotional independence from parents and other adults.* Up to this point, children have depended on parents for love, praise, and tenderness. Now they must develop understanding and respect for their parents without the emotional dependence. Peer interaction facilitates this growth, but it is a slow process and need not be an abrupt happening.
- *Selecting and preparing for an occupation.* One of the main goals for the adolescent is to decide what to do with his or her life vocationally, and then get ready to do it. This task is becoming increasingly more difficult as our economy changes and industry progresses to its present level of automation.
- *Preparing for marriage and family life.* Today, patterns of marriage and family living are being readjusted to the changing economic, social, and religious characteristics of society. Educational demands put off marriage for some, while encouraging marriage in others. Living together and trial marriages have developed to challenge traditional concepts.

- *Desiring and achieving socially responsible behavior.* Sweeping changes in lifestyles, especially in the area of marriage and family life, have clouded this task for the adolescent. Society now provides numerous models of apparently "socially acceptable behavior" involving cohabitation, communal living, and other varieties of hetero- and homosexual behavior.
- *Acquiring a set of values and an ethical system as a guide to behavior.* Throughout childhood, the individual is educated into the parental value system. As an adolescent, the individual's values are tested outside the family circle. Then, the adolescent must either accept or reject family teachings, but rejection demands that an alternative be found. Through this method, the adolescent assembles his or her personal value system and philosophy of life.

### Psychoanalytical Theorists: Erik Erikson and James Marcia

Erikson's theory of adolescence drew heavily upon the work of Sigmund Freud, but resulted in a more practical application. Erikson described eight stages of human development. In each stage the individual must confront a conflict area exclusive to the stage. The confrontation produces one of two totally different reactions. One is positive; the other negative. Obviously a negative reaction produces problems and impedes progress to the next stage.

For the adolescent, Erikson labeled the task—identity versus identity confusion. The real effort here is to establish a sense of personal identity, since the individual has dealt with identity crises prior to the adolescent years. Erikson feels that during adolescence there must be an integration of converging identity elements and a resolution of conflict that he divided into seven major parts.[8] In the following, the seven parts of the conflict are expressed as bipolar tendencies.

- *Temporal perspective versus time confusion.* Adolescents must develop a stable concept of time as it relates to their changing self and their eventual position in adult society. They must be able to coordinate the past and the future so they can understand how long it takes to find their own sense of life plans.

- *Self-certainty versus self-consciousness.* Adolescents must develop self-confidence based on experiences so they can believe in themselves and feel that they have a reasonable chance to accomplish future goals. Self-image and social relationships play important roles in the accomplishment of this task.
- *Role experimentation versus role fixation.* In an attempt to discover who he or she is, the adolescent discovers many things that he or she is not. Adolescents can experiment with many different identities, personalities, ideas, philosophies, and ways of walking and talking. Identity emerges because of the experimentation. The goal is to reject the negative roles experimented with and adopt the most positive role possible.
- *Apprenticeship versus work paralysis.* The goal of this task is to lead the adolescent toward focusing on productive involvement in a vocation and reject inactivity. The adolescent must begin to experiment or entertain ideas of possible avenues of life works.
- *Sexual identity versus bisexual confusion.* Resolving the sexual identity crises involves identifying with an appropriate sex role and rejecting bisexual tendencies. Developing a clear identification with one sex or the other is an important basis for future heterosexual intimacy and as a basis for a firm identity.
- *Leadership polarization versus authority diffusion.* Adolescents must become aware of their leadership potential or their lack of it. There are times when the adolescent must lead, and there are times where he or she must be led. A willingness to be open to whichever situation exists for the young person is important.
- *Ideological commitment versus confusion of ideals.* This conflict is closely related to all of the others because a value system, or lack of it, conditions how the adolescent deals with the other six areas of conflict. As our society becomes more lax in its standards, it becomes increasingly harder for young people to get a clear picture of ideals and make commitments.

Many studies have followed Erikson's in attempting to deal with the identity of adolescents. James Marcia provides a very useful description of adolescent identity employing the words *crisis* and *commitment.*[9] Not to be considered in their normal context, these words have an expanded meaning as we look at adolescent identity. The word *crisis* is understood to mean any conflict encountered by the adolescent with respect to identity. *Commitment* is understood to mean any resolution to the previously mentioned types of crisis. Within this framework, it is possible to develop four areas of identity status. These are numbered because they are, within limits, sequential. They will also serve as a foundation in the following section on the spiritual development of the adolescent.

*1. Identity Confusion.* The adolescent in this state has not had any identity crisis and has made no commitment. No crisis/no commitment. They have not thought seriously about a possible occupation and are not too concerned about it. They seem to be uninterested in ideological matters or feel one view is as good as the other. "Withdrawal" seems to be the best word to characterize this stage.

*2. Identity Foreclosure.* The adolescent in this state is committed, but has not experienced a crisis. No crisis/no commitment. The most common examples of foreclosure involve individuals whose political, religious, and vocational decisions have essentially been made for them by their parents, or sometimes by their peers. They become what others intend them to become, without really deciding for themselves. Their security lies in avoiding change or stress.

*3. Identity Moratorium.* The adolescent in this state has experienced crisis but has made no commitment. Crisis/no commitment. A time of moratorium is extremely important for the adolescent. As defined by Erikson, it is that period when the adolescent is clearly neither a child nor an adult. This stage is the time for the adolescent to question what types of commitments he or she will make when faced with the multitude of crises that he or she will experience.

*4. Identity Achievement.* The adolescent in this state has experienced different crises and has made various commitments. Crisis/commitment. He or she has a stable self-definition, has committed to a course of preparation or has prepared for a vocation, and understands his or her opportunities and limitations.

In summary, in the first instance, the adolescent does not know who he or she is, and does not really think about it (identity confusion); in the second, identity has been imposed on the adolescent either by parents or sometimes by the state (foreclosure); in the third, the adolescent is trying to discover who he or she can and will be (moratorium); in the last instance, the adolescent has achieved an identity (identity achievement).[10] These last three stages are helpful in understanding the spiritual development of the adolescent.

### Cognitive Theorists: Jean Piaget and David Elkind

Piaget was probably the best known and by far the most influential of all cognitive theorists. He divided the stages of cognitive development into four major parts. Sensorimotor and preoperational stages generally cover from birth through seven years of age. The adolescent years come into focus during the latter half of the third stage (concrete operational) and all of the fourth stage (formal operational). The concrete operational stage has an age range of eleven years old to fourteen or fifteen years old and deals with propositional thinking and the ability to deal with the hypothetical. Piaget was quick to point out that these ages were only an approximation. In fact, some recent testing of college freshmen revealed that only about half of them had reached formal operational thinking. This is somewhat of an indictment of secondary education in the school systems around the country.

David Elkind, a prominent Piagetian psychologist, brought into focus the concept of adolescent egocentrism when he suggested that egocentrism may be a "bridge between the study of cognitive structure on the one hand and the exploration of personality dynamics" on the other. The adolescent must learn to distinguish between the thoughts of other people and his or her own. Because the adolescent is so preoccupied with his or her own behavior, he or she believes that others are, also. This egocentrism can lead to two characteristics of adolescent behavior: the construction of an "imaginary audience" and the creation of a "personal fable." The imaginary audience influence causes the adolescent to feel as if he or she is on "stage" or constantly being watched. Because he or she makes up this audience, the audience knows everything he or she knows—all of his or her personal shortcomings and problems. The personal fable influence can cause the adolescent to feel that his or her experience is totally unique and that no one has ever been this good or this bad off.

The imaginary audience gradually gives way to the real audience, and the personal fable gives way to a deeper understanding of reality. And with a greater grasp of reality, adolescent egocentrism fades and adulthood begins to emerge in the healthy adolescent. (Even though Elkind's books—*The Hurried Child* (1981) and *All Dressed Up & No Place to Go* (1984) are dated, the concepts are excellent and still appropriate.)

## THEORIES IN PRACTICE: MINISTRY ISSUES

The first part of this chapter has been an attempt to *briefly* deal with some *lengthy* theories as a means of introducing the reader to the different views of adolescent development. The next section of this chapter deals with practical applications and considerations of the previously mentioned theories.

The adolescent functions in a variety of "worlds," including school, home, the peer group, and hopefully the church. In many cases, the adolescent is a somewhat different person in each world. As a result of this, a schoolteacher might think the adolescent is beyond hope. Adding to the confusion in all of this is the application of Gesell's "spiral growth theory," which has a roller coaster effect on the behavior and attitude of the adolescent. In Gesell's theory, all the even years were peaceful while the odd-numbered years were turbulent. Thus a good year was followed by a bad year. This might help explain to that Sunday school teacher in the ninth and tenth grade department why the tenth graders seem like different people than they were as ninth graders. There are also those current "theorists," this writer included, who think the "spiral" is an active theory still in effect but each year is shortened to several months. This means you still have the forward movement followed by the backward "regrouping" or assimilating, but the complete cycle happens several times in a year rather than just once. In addition, this further complicates things for the teacher and the parent.

Obviously, many environmental factors come into play at this point. All of the "worlds" at this time are with the sphere of influence. Maybe the best advice to parents, teachers, and youth workers during this time would be to be a little more tolerant and understanding of the "bad months/years" and a little more appreciative and encouraging during the "good months/years."

It is not totally unheard of for an adolescent to experience very little of the up-down, good-bad syndrome, but it is very unusual. When it does happen like that, some research has indicated that later in life the adolescent, now an adult, experiences the roller coaster effect and it happens at a time that is not nearly as acceptable as it would have been during adolescent years.

Of major concern during development is the adolescent's search for identity and a strengthening of his or her self-image. Merton Strommen, in his book *Five Cries of Youth*, stated that almost three-fourths of all young people are struggling with low self-esteem at one time or another.

A good, positive self-image is a must for an adolescent and it might well be the hardest thing for the adolescent to achieve. As young people function in the world, they watch television, go to movies, read magazines, and they see other young people and young adults. But the others they see are models and movie stars, and they don't look like that. So because they don't look or act like the models and the movie stars, something must be wrong with them. They are not alright because they don't measure up. Also, life doesn't go as smoothly as in the movies or on television, so something must be wrong with the adolescent. Adolescents may or may not understand with their heads that it's "make believe," but they rarely understand with their hearts that what they see is not real.

Physical appearance and beauty are not at their peak for the adolescent during junior high or early senior high. They do not look as good as the young stars they see on the screen and on the tube. They also don't realize that in many cases the stars "portraying" adolescents are actually in their mid-twenties and "finished" with all of the appearance problems related to adolescent years. The problems with skin, hair, teeth, voice, and weight don't help the self-image situation either. The adolescent is undergoing a tremendous amount of physiological changes, many of which affect outward appearance. Either too much or too little of anything appearance-wise at this time can be devastating. The key words seem to be normal and average, both of which adolescents are not.

Another situation that does not help self-image at all is that the adolescent thinks the internal struggle that he or she is going through is reflected on the outside. In other words, because he or she looks bad on the inside to himself or herself, the adolescent thinks he or she looks bad on the outside to others.

In dealing with problems of self-image, the mandate is twofold: help the adolescent know and understand that he or she is not a finished product and go to great lengths to avoid calling attention to his or her appearance. Do not get caught up in the popular pastime among young people of putting each other down. It's acceptable (acceptable, not healthy) for them to put each other down, but not for an adult to do it. The put down is one of the all-time classic defense mechanisms; if you make somebody else look bad it helps you look just a little bit better. But it should be taboo for the adult.

With regard to the finished product, remind young people that the adolescent years are like practice for the big game—life. It's OK to make mistakes and mess up in practice—that's what it's for. The important thing is the game—life. However, because the adolescent lives in the "now," care should be taken not to dwell too much on the future or the fact that it's going to get better. The young person wants help for right now—today!

Developing a value system is of prime importance to the adolescent because that will be the guideline for living and functioning in the world. Parents, ministers, and other Christian adults make contributions and influence this system, but so does the peer group. The family, for most young people up to this point, has been of primary importance. However, as the adolescent years emerge, the family moves from primary status to secondary status, and the peer group moves into the primary slot. What the peer group thinks and does becomes a major influence. Parents, especially, should be aware of this and not resent it. They should, however, be concerned about the company their young people keep. Parents should be encouraged to meet and get to know the child's friends and their families.

A value system and identity are closely linked, and during this time a real dilemma for parents and even ministers comes into focus. As an adolescent seeks to develop an identity, according to Marcia, he or she moves through stages of confusion, foreclosure, and moratorium on the way to achievement. Foreclosure, as previously mentioned, is an almost automatic adoption of parental values and commitments. The move into moratorium is a time to question and evaluate and reevaluate and have a time where there are no real commitments. The young person must have this time of searching in order to progress to the achieved identity stage. The true dilemma for the parents and those who would minister to the young person surfaces at this point. The following questions have to be considered: Do you really allow your young person to experience moratorium or do you try to prevent it? Do you allow moratorium but ignore it? Do you allow moratorium in all areas but religious development?

The only concrete answer to the previous questions is that it is virtually impossible to prevent moratorium. All young people will experience moratorium in some form or another. There will also be varying degrees of involvement in moratorium. Some adolescents pass through it only slightly inconvenienced, while others are almost devastated by it.

In the area of relationships with parents and other adults, it is helpful to consider that an adult personality and an adolescent personality are very different. While not all adults and not all adolescents fall into the following types, the comparisons do show distinct differences that can lead to disagreements.[11]

- Adults are cautious, based on experience; the adolescent is daring and willing to try new things, but lacks judgment based on experience.
- Adults are oriented to the past and compare the present with the way things used to be; the adolescent's only reality is the present. The past is irrelevant and the future is dim and uncertain.
- Adults are realistic and sometimes cynical about life and people; the adolescent is idealistic and optimistic.
- Adults are conservative in manners, morals, and mores; the adolescent challenges traditional codes and ethics and experiments with new ideas and lifestyles.
- Adults are generally contented, satisfied, and resigned to the status quo; the adolescent is critical, restless, and somewhat unhappy with the way things are.
- Adults want to stay young and sometimes fear age; the adolescent wants to be grown-up, but never wants to become old.

The personal fable and the imaginary audience were mentioned earlier in this chapter. Much of the discipline problems with young people, especially in groups, can be attributed to the imaginary audience theory. Adolescents think that wherever they go and whatever they do, all eyes are on them, so they cover their true self by acting out. If they show the world a real tough guy or gal, people might not see the sensitive adolescent underneath. If he or she shows the world the rude, abrasive adolescent, people might not see the sensitive adolescent underneath. The first question in most discipline problems is what is trying to be hidden or covered up.

The personal fable has two somewhat different manifestations. On one hand, the adolescent feels that no one else in the world is having the same problems he or he is having. No one else has a terrible complexion. No one else is too tall for their weight. No one else has a body odor problem. No one else's hair grows in four different directions. On the other hand, the personal fable manifestation gives young people a sense of invincibility or immortality. Death and sickness can't touch them because they are not like everyone else. These young people are hit really hard when close friends or family members are lost.

Perhaps the best way to deal with the imaginary audience and personal fable is to endure it. As the adolescent matures and begins to develop a stronger sense of reality, both of these areas seem to ease off and cease to be a problem.

Development of the adolescent's sexuality and interest in the opposite sex are major influences in his or her daily functioning. Anyone working with young people needs to diligently research both of these subjects. The tragedy is that if adults wait until adolescence to begin discussing sexuality and sexual development, it is much too late. Middle- and upper-elementary years are the times to deal with this issue.

In most cases, interest in the opposite sex will come during upper-elementary years for girls and just a little later than that for boys. It is generally agreed that girls are one to two years ahead of boys physiologically and socially. Boys do not seem to catch up until around age fourteen or fifteen. This is one reason that coeducational classes at the junior-high level of Sunday school present problems. A seventh-grade girl and a seventh-grade boy are two different people. The seventh-grade boy may just be beginning to think about girls, while the seventh-grade girl is already looking at boys. But she is looking at ninth-grade boys and not the seventh-grade boys who are her own age. This is obviously an oversimplification, but it emphasizes the point that a social and physical gap exists in the junior-high years.

## SPIRITUAL DEVELOPMENT

Our Christian faith is based on developing a *personal* relationship with Jesus Christ. For the adolescent, it is a personal walk—a personal encounter with the living Christ. It is difficult, if not impossible, to describe how each person's faith will develop during the adolescent years. So this last section will be an attempt to furnish a "backdrop" for acquiring a general view of how the adolescent personality responds to its surroundings and influences as the faith and value system begins and/or develops.

Marcia's identity stages of *foreclosure, moratorium,* and *achievement* are helpful in looking at this spiritual progression. Ministers and Christian parents teach that there are certain truths and certain standards that we uphold and adhere to and so must our adolescents. During *foreclosure* this poses no problem. Parental standards are readily accepted. But as the young person (older child) begins to move into the peer group and his or her "world," things don't seem that well defined. Things begin to look more fuzzy than clear. Adolescents begin to say that maybe they need to see for themselves and experience some things before they accept them. Maybe they will adopt the same beliefs as their parents, but they want to base their acceptance on their own involvement and experiences rather than someone else's.

One dictionary defines *moratorium* as a waiting period set by an authority. A second definition lists it as a legally authorized period of delay in the performance of a legal obligation. For the adolescent, it means a delay in the adoption of someone else's values or beliefs until they can make a decision of their own and feel good about it. The areas of decisions they face during this time are almost incalculable. The spiritual decisions are the most important ones they will face on their way through *moratorium* to *achievement.*

A good example of the move through *foreclosure, moratorium,* and *achievement* is illustrated in the following story. The names are fictitious, but the story is true. "Scott" is sixteen years old. He grew up in a Christian home. He has been in church since he was an infant. His parents love him very much and have been supportive of the interests that Scott has had. He made a public profession of faith in Christ when he was baptized at age nine. During his late junior high and early high school years, Scott began to make some bad choices. Not because his parents didn't love him, not because he was mad at them, not because he was trying to prove a point, and not because he wasn't supported and encouraged. He just started through the "wide gate" and "down the broad path" that Jesus talked about in Matthew 7:13-14. That path leads to destruction and he was on the way. Then Scott was promoted into John's Sunday school class. John was one of those teachers who really cared about his class members and got involved in their lives. He and Scott really connected. John helped Scott hear the same things his parents were saying to him, which were also the same things previous teachers and caring adults had said to him. In time, Scott renewed his commitment to Christ. He still struggles with the same temptations that any sixteen-year-old does. One of his favorite passages is I Peter 5:8-9 (NIV). Scott knows that the devil is "prowling around like a roaring lion looking for someone to devour." He is moving through *moratorium,* but Scott still has rough times. He will make other bad choices, just as we all do.

Not all young people will have a rough time on their spiritual journey. They will have to come to their own conclusions, however, about what they believe, why they believe it, how it will impact their lives, and what difference the belief will make in their lives.

What can parents do to help in their young person's spiritual journey? One of the most effective ways to teach is by example. They can model the life of discipleship. They can provide the best possible atmosphere for discussion while still retaining discipline and a loving, caring attitude. They can create a safe place to ask questions and explore biblical truths together. They can approach specific passages with their own view being expressed while staying open to a slightly different view from their young person.

In his book *Understanding Today's Youth Culture,* Walt Mueller discusses ten strategies that parents can use in dealing with negative peer pressure. They are also effective in facilitating a young person's journey. Included in his strategies are:

- Actively helping them to build a God-centered self-image
- Helping them to learn by asking them good questions
- Opening up your home to your young person's friends
- Giving your young person the opportunity to make his or her own choices within clearly defined boundaries
- Not being afraid to draw the line and say NO!
- PRAY, PRAY, PRAY!"[11]

Perhaps one of the most difficult actions parents have to take is to release their young person at the appropriate time. You have them for such a short while, you want them to adopt and adhere to strong spiritual principles, but you know they will begin to make spiritual decisions on their own. You know that those decisions will have a life-changing impact. You hope and pray that you have said and done the right things and then you pray that your young person will become open to the power of the Holy Spirit for leadership and guidance throughout life.

Growing up at any time is tough, but never so tough a time as now. A key word for parents, ministers, and anyone else working with adolescents is *survival*. Help young people survive adolescence intact. It can be done with love, care, and understanding. Many survive without that, but they are often confused and alienated.

It is also tough trying to parent and minister to this age group. It is unfortunate that we cannot see how the Master Teacher spent this time, but we have no biblical account of the adolescent years of our Lord. Too bad! We could have learned a lot.

## ADDITIONAL COMMENTS

The preadolescent and adolescent years—more specifically the years from fifth grade through the senior year in high school—are more susceptible or vulnerable to cultural changes than any other years. Adolescents are more influenced by the changes in fashion, music, television, movies, magazines, school, their peer group, and the "latest fad," than any other age. For this reason, it is imperative for anyone who works with this age group to stay current on the latest "happenings" and changes. If possible and appropriate, watch an episode every now and then of the most popular teen television shows and several scenes from their favorite movies. You may not be able to sit through the whole show, but watch just enough to grasp the premise or theme of the young person's world. When possible, try to listen for a minute or two to some of their music. You will become aware of the type of influence that this music can exert upon the young people who are exposed to it. Urge parents to pay close attention to what their young people are listening to and seeing. Such knowledge will ensure parental effectiveness in dealing with these issues and in helping the young people.

Perhaps the easiest way to find out what is happening in the young person's world is to establish a relationship with young people and talk to them. If they feel comfortable and "safe," you can gain tremendous insight about the way they think and about the issues that affect and influence them.

## NOTES

1. Dacey, John S. *Adolescents Today*. Glenview, IL: Scott, Foresman and Co., 1986, pp. 4-5.

2. Havighurst, Robert J. *Developmental Tasks and Education*. New York: David McKay Co., Inc., 1952, p. 33. Havighurst's developmental tasks were originally published in pamphlet form in 1948 by the University of Chicago, for use in his classes. The five tasks listed here from Havighurst's original list were considered to be part of the adolescent experience. Forty-plus years later they can be used as markers for someone who has already moved out of the adolescent period.

3. LeFrancois, Guy R. *Adolescents*. Belmont, CA: Wadsworth Publishing Co., 1981, p. 108. This book is no longer in print, but it would be worth the effort of finding because of LeFrancois' unique sense of humor in dealing with the youth culture. It was used as a main textbook in adolescent psychology classes at colleges and universities through the mid-1980s.

4. Ibid.

5. Ibid., p. 111.

6. Gesell, Arnold, Frances Ilg, and Louise Ames. *Youth: The Years from Ten to Sixteen*. New York: Harper and Row Publishers, 1956. This book is also out of print. It completed a trilogy of books that began with the publication of *Infant and Child in the Culture of Today* (1943) followed by *The Child from Five to Ten* (1946). Most of the study of the young people from ten to sixteen were made under the auspices of the Gesell Institute of Child Development, founded in 1950.

7. Rice, F. Philip. *The Adolescent*. Boston: Allyn and Bacon, Inc., 1987, p. 111.

8. Ibid., p. 94.

9. Marcia, James E. "Ego Identity Status: Relationship to Change in Self-Esteem, General Maladjustment, and Authoritarianism," *Journal of Personality*, 35, pp. 118-133, 1967.

10. LeFrancois, p. 134.

11. This is an adaptation from W. J. Anderson's *Design for Family Living*. Minneapolis: T. S. Denison and Co., 1964; and quoted from F. Philip Rice's *The Adolescent*. Boston: Allyn and Bacon, Inc., 1987.

12. Mueller, Walt. *Understanding Today's Youth Culture*. Wheaton, IL: Tyndale House Publishers, Inc., 1994, pp. 200-208.

## ANNOTATED BIBLIOGRAPHY

Barna, George. *Generation Next: What You Need to Know About Today's Youth*. Ventura, CA: Regal Books, 1995.

Barna gives a statistical look at Generation X. He focuses on those members of Generation X who are currently youth. His information is gathered through phone interview research with 723 youths nationwide. Barna covers most of the major areas related to youth culture.

Benson, Peter L., Judy Galbraith, and Pamela Espeland. *What Kids Need to Succeed*. Minneapolis, MN: Free Spirit Publishing, Inc., 1995.

This book is a compilation of basic characteristics or attributes that young people of today need to succeed in life. The work is based on a nationwide survey of 273,000 youths from 600 communities and thirty-three states. This group of authors identified thirty "assets," sixteen of which are external and can be nourished by caring, principled adults.

Ford, Kevin Graham. *Jesus for a New Generation*. Downings Grove, IL: Intervarsity Press, 1995.

Ford presents a compelling look at the generation of the American population commonly referred to as Generation X, Baby Busters, or the Thirteenth Generation. He examines the culture this generation has grown up in and how they are living today. It is a good introduction to the generation of adolescents growing up in the late nineties and the beginning of the next century.

Mueller, Walt. *Understanding Today's Youth Culture*. Wheaton, IL: Tyndale House Publishers, Inc. 1994.

This book is directed toward youth workers, teachers, parents, and anyone else who works with young people. It's goal is to "help you understand and address the complex interplay between the cultural forces that are molding and shaping the values, attitudes, and behaviors of the kids under your care." Mueller covers such topics as understanding the media and music that surround teens, teenage substance abuse, depression, and spirituality.

Santrock, John W. *Adolescence,* Seventh Edition. New York: McGraw-Hill, 1998.

This is a general textbook for the study of adolescence at the college or graduate level. It covers a wide variety of issues relating to youth culture. It provides valuable insight into the developmental stages of adolescent development.

Strommen, Merton P. and A. Irene Strommen. *Five Cries of Parents.* San Francisco: Harper and Row Publishers, 1984; and Strommen, Merton P. *Five Cries of Youth.* San Francisco: Harper and Row, 1988.

These books were listed together because they are best read as companions to each other. These books are somewhat dated, but much of the material is as applicable today as it was ten years ago. In many circles, Merton Strommen is considered a pioneer in the area of adolescent research that he built around surveys.

Chapter 4

# Young Adulthood:
# Starting on Their Own

Thom Meigs

## WILDERNESS AND PROMISE:
## GENERATION X AND BEYOND

Consider these thoughts. Young people who were born in the late 1970s to 1980 have always known a world affected by HIV and AIDS. They may have vaguely heard of an 8-track tape. Few have lived in a household without an answering machine. They now have mobile phones. Few have ever used a television set with only five channels.

A young adult who is now between the ages of twenty-three to thirty-three, probably wore Izod, especially windbreakers that folded up (into a pouch) that he or she could wear around the waist. He or she owned something Jordache; actually knows who Rick Springfield, Cyndi Lauper, and Bo and Luke Duke are; dressed to emulate a person seen idolized in entertainment or sports; learned to swim about the same time the movie *Jaws* came out; used the phrase "kiss mah grits" in conversation; knows who shot J.R.; perhaps had a Dorothy Hamill haircut; actually laughed at the ad phrase, "Where's the beef?"; was intently glued to watch Laura and Luke's wedding; and owned a pair of rainbow suspenders like the ones Mork wore.

Young adults today have inherited labels, attempts to gain understanding of them, such as Generation X, "Baby Busters," "The Free Generation," "Twenty-Somethings," "The Repair Generation," and others. All of these labels have been attached to a generation that abhors labels. They have grown up in a postmodern (whatever that means), Internet, digital, techno-computerized world that affects how they spend their time and energy, and consequently effects relationship strengths and deficiencies. They struggle with the tension of strong self-absorption and awareness of others.

The word *adult* interestingly comes from the Latin *adolescere*, which means "to grow up." The word itself is neutral about the nature of the growth. However, *adolescere* does imply *process* more than the *possession* of a special status, or particular capacity. In this sense, however "grown up" Angela and Chris (imaginary young adults) feel about their years of development, they cannot realistically think of themselves as totally completed persons yet.

The young adult is very much a "wayfarer" or "pilgrim," engaging a sense of "wilderness wandering" and yet full, of "promise."[1] Accepting their "givens" of life, a central question is posed, *What would you like your life to be like from now on?* Ziggy, the comic strip character was advised, "There is nothing medical science can do about your condition! I recommend that you have your cartoonist redraw you!" Since that option is ill-advised and a return to a factory drawing is out of order, let us try to create a positive and valued profile of the young adult.

## FLOWING FEATURES
## OF YOUNG ADULTHOOD

What is it like to be a "normal" young adult? What happens characteristically during this transitional era? We know for one thing that Angela and Chris are no longer simply dependent *apprentices* on their family, church, educational systems, and peer groups/subcultures. What emerges, among other things, is their capacity to attain an identity that includes physical maturation, the ability to live intimately with a person of the opposite sex, and hopefully, to become well-integrated. They have reached a decisive crossroads in their journey of life.

### Crucial Turning Points

The word *crisis* can mean a "dividing time." Young adulthood is a normal time of crisis—whether to move forward and ahead, to go backward to the way it was, or even to stagnate as if one were in a whirlpool of accumulated experiences. A crisis experience is a non-surprising tension between our aspirations and hopes on the one hand, and our finitude/limitations and vulnerabilities on the other. Crises can be moments of achievement and celebration. They *confront* us with issues of truth, integrity, mercy, and responsibility for actions; and *fortify* us in giving "heart," encouragement, and affirmation. There can also be tough moments of hard adjustment. Hopefully, as young adults Angela and Chris can effectively utilize their opportunities and teachable moments, as well as accept and claim the responsibilities that accompany them. Thus, the growing up continues.

A young adult's energies, interests, and aspirations can be directed outward beyond his or her own individual growth and development. In a sense, young adults are able to start "sailing" on their own, for, by and large, Angela and Chris have been taught "to navigate and . . . been provided with charts albeit they are charts that can be only approximately correct, for the currents and reefs change constantly."[2]

If there has been faithful, even skilled, modeling in the church and at home, one of the tasks that Chris has learned is how to accept consequences of his decisions, including how the decision is processed, whom he chooses as his confidants and consultants, and when other persons become involved, such as a pastor, a spiritual leader, or a teacher. Theodore Lidz's insight about the young adult may hold true, "Usually he asks another to share the journey, and soon others join them, bidden and unbidden, and their welfare depends upon his skills and stability."[3]

*Camera Over Here*

Our life's filming tends to take place in relatively predictable steps or stages. Adaptation to change is a continual facet of life's movement. The film has been rolling. For example, the stage you've left behind has been called "adolescence." As a "moving into the next layer" of experience, you have grown or matured physically and biologically. You're aware of these changes and shapings. The way in which you relate to and view your body is very important. For example, *do you sense indeed that your body is a well-intended gift from God, to be claimed and taken care of in appropriate goodness?*

Our individual development doesn't take place in a vacuum. It has context. We hope it has been a "people-making" context. It has depended on the support and nurture received from family, the quality of inspiration, challenge, and scripting of family, school/education, neighborhood, peers, workplace, government, and religious affiliation. Sometimes that nurturance is lacking. Young adulthood gives a "near-to" opportunity to reflect one's experience and behavior. Part of Chris and Angela's tug-of-war is a desire to look or skip ahead, while feeling a strong urge to look over their shoulders at the past.

Family history indeed is something like an "iceberg." Most of us are aware of only a small percentage (the tip) of what actually went on. It does help, however, to discover the feelings, rules, and patterns that were interwoven into our family's fabric. Virginia Satir and others suggest that the family is the "factory" where persons are "made." "You, the adults, are the 'peoplemakers.'"[4] The Christian faith would add that the spirit of God is the change agent.

*Family Threads*

Chris and Angela need to assess what their own family was like to recognize what differences they want to make for themselves. It may mean they will confirm some of the family's strengths. Learning to praise those strengths is a sign of maturing. The point of departure that begins, "What is wrong with your upbringing?" is reframed to a positive sense of thanksgiving.

Four significant threads of family life surface, in both *troubled* or *nurturing* families, according to Virginia Satir. These threads, whether present or absent, include: (1) self-worth—the concepts and feelings you have about yourself; (2) communication—the ways persons in the system work out the meaning each other has for the other; (3) rules—the guidance and structures for how you feel and act; and (4) connection to larger society—the ways and strategies by which the family relates to other people and institutions.[5]

Troubled families know more about the language of fear and anxiety than the language of faith and trust. Self-worth is low or deflated. Communication is indirect, assumptive, circumventing, and sometimes dishonest. Rules are very tight, hierarchical, non-negotiable with a sense of the everlasting. The connection to society is fearful, blaming, or placating.

On the other hand, nurturing families are interested in the language of faith and trust that includes the ability to say to each other, "There is no reason for us to be afraid of each other." Self-worth is high and expansive. Communication is clear, nonassumptive, and honest. Rules are certainly necessary, but they show flexibility, appropriateness, ability to change, and humanness. The connection to society is discerning, yet open and hopeful.

Every person has feelings of *worth*, either positive or negative. "Which is it for you?" We all *communicate*. The basic question is, however, "How do we communicate consistently, and what happens as a result of our communication?" We all have *rules* that we follow. "What kind are they, and how well do they work for us?" We are *interfaced with society*. "How are we linked, and what happens as a result of the relatedness?"[6]

*Friend or Foe?*

By now, we see that young adulthood is a "role of challenge." Young adults are moving toward greater complexity, competence, and integration[7] from the challenges, support, and experiences they've brought with them to this point. It is a complex process for Chris and Angela, as it is for all of us, to assimilate their thoughts, feelings, values, dreams, aspirations, choices, behaviors, and beliefs. As Angela said after completing graduate school, "It's not getting any easier or simpler. It's a bigger world out here and inside me than I had stopped to imagine."

What specific developmental issues are they currently struggling with? What *life-giving*, rather than *life-extracting*, skills and knowledge are called for by these challenges? "Are helpful resources available to me?" "Does the future act as my friend?" The question is not simply "Who am I now?" but also *quo vadis*, "Where do I go from here?"

Levinson coined the term "the novice phase" for the youth-to-early-adult transition, beginning about age seventeen and continuing until about age thirty-three. How would you respond to his insistence that "a young man needs about fifteen years to emerge from adolescence, find his place in adult society, and commit himself to a more stable life?"[8] Levinson's "novice phase" has three "developmental bridges," each with its own tasks: the early adult transition (roughly ages seventeen to twenty-two); entering the adult world (ages twenty-two to twenty-eight); and the dramatic age thirty transition. Together, they serve a singular function: "the process of entry into adulthood." However, remember that the actual time or "event-izing" when adult life begins cannot be simply set chronologically. It can be a bit elusive. Trying to draw exact, visible lines of age boundaries between when young adulthood begins and ends is an uneasy business. Lucien Coleman suggested, "Trying to define these boundaries with *precision* is something like attempting to locate a state line on a rural road where there is no marker.[9] The clues may lie more in the subtle psychological and sociological changes, occurring *intra*personally and *inter*personally. An illustration of this is the person who engaged both a vocational/career choice and a mate while in late adolescence.

## Saying Good-Bye Thankfully to the Preadult World

The early adult transition challenges Chris and Angela to say a creative "good-bye" to the adolescent structure and to take preliminary, preparatory steps into the adult world. It is a rite of passage for them. It includes how they both separate from and yet claim family origin and heritage.

Do you remember the way your life differed after high school from life during the high school years? If college was part of the experience, you were on your own in ways that do not correspond to high school. Do you remember some of those differences and the things that surprised you? You were expected to manage your behavior both inside and outside the classroom in order to accomplish the academic goals you had set.

If you did not go on to college, you were still expected to learn life management skills. Whereas the college student made decisions about courses and curriculum, noncollege persons made decisions about full-time work. Nevertheless, a part of the ongoing challenge of these years is the issue, "What's ahead? Will the future offer a sense of welcome and a feeling of 'come on ahead; you can trust me?'"

*A Network of Influences*

There are at least four levels of the social world in which your development takes place:

1. Immediate personal settings, such as family and friends.
2. The network of personal settings and how these have influenced you.
3. Large institutions and organizations.
4. Culture that permeates and influences all levels of these systems.[10]

These systems require balancing acts in terms of the demands placed upon you. A friend of Angela's shared with me, "I find it difficult to parcel out my time. I find I am constantly forcing myself to decide between being with my friends and getting my work done. My emotional filter system gets clogged up with dust at times." Stress has to do both with your expectations and actual experiences. If there is a differential between what one actually "expects" to be happening (wants to be occurring) and what one is actually "experiencing," that difference means stress. The demands outweigh or imbalance our perceived resources to handle it.

*Getting into Formation*

In Levinson's "provisional" or "novice" phase, young men especially, face four basic tasks:

1. Forming and living out a "dream," which is "a vague sense of self-in-adult-world" and fitting it into your "life structure,"
2. Forming mentor or teachable/learning relationships with significant others who can guide, advise, and facilitate the realization of the "dream,"
3. Forming an occupation or pursuing a career as a way of life, while enhancing skills and credentials,
4. Developing and forming intimate relationships.

This fourth task explores the meaning of love in marriage and family, establishing a basis for affection, emotional disclosure or intimacy, sexuality, respect for authority, friendship, and enduring commitment.[11] None of these tasks will be finished before the end of this phase. These tasks tend to "plug along" unevenly, with recurrent ups and downs.

Between the ages of seventeen and twenty-two, most people are either building or need to take time to build a framework for leaving home and family, and to channel a preliminary leap into an independent adult world. Although it can be traumatic for some, most people experience what Levinson calls a "voice within," which speaks to us about "changing" life—building or modifying, excluding or adding, starting or leaving, dismantling or installing, nurturing, or combinations of these.

In *Passages*, Gail Sheehy defines three basic types of women. The "caregivers" ("nurturants") seek meaning and value from giving to others, and at this time in their twenties are not torn over going beyond or extending the domestic role. The "either/ors" choose either nurturant roles or work/accomplishment roles. The "integrators" ("Super women") are those who try to combine marriage, career, and motherhood in their twenties.[12] Young adult, how would you respond to or alter those types? Are they accurate? What would you change or eliminate about her types?

*Morning Has Broken*

To be or not to be more self-directed is at least part of the question for the young adult. Learning the value of "mutuality" is another part of the question. The value of self-direction emerges as a kind of call to take initiative about one's own life.

Mutuality means the willingness of persons to invest themselves in one another's lives, with the purpose of helping to build up each other in care and growth and not to tear down and destroy. It is wanting for the other as much as you want for yourself. In the New Testament, the word koinonia, commonly translated as "fellowship," means in a rooted sense "the equipping of each other for service together in Christ." This is a word that attempts to shorten relational distance and bring persons closer together. Strongly competitive models discourage and disengage you from others. The apostle Paul expressed the difference when he reminded Christians in Philippi that they are partners/partakers in grace and not rivals in spirit. Categories of "winners" and "losers" promote unhealthy tensions of comparison between persons.

Mutuality is a "good news" word. But it will sometimes "scare the daylights" out of us. Let me illustrate selectively by referring again to Egan and Cowan's interpretation of mutuality:

1. Disclosing and sharing yourself with others in a game-free way when such disclosure is appropriate,
2. Listening to others carefully and trying to understand their point of view. . .
3. Engaging in nondefensive self-exploration when challenged. . .[13]

The dawning of new mornings and days prompts some personal reflections. For example, "What am I accomplishing, and at what cost?" "What kind of support do I usually look for from other people?" "What adjectives do I believe describe the important dimensions of myself?" "What are three things I seem to do well?" "What is one relationship in my life I would hate to lose?" "What do I think or hope that I will be doing five years from now?"

## Never Too Young to Grieve

A weight-challenged and confused young person was conversing about his tennis game with a friend. "When my opponent hits the ball to me, my brain immediately barks out a command to my body: 'Race up to the net,' it says. 'Slam a blistering drive to the far corner of the court, jump back into the position to return the next volley.' Then my body says, 'Who . . . me?'"

The following sections incorporate a number of characteristics of a normal transitional period that begins with "Who . . . me?" and moves to a more "in-sight-ful" response, "Yes . . . this is probably me!" or "This could be me!"

First, the young adult may at times feel suspended between the past and the future. Girl or woman? Boy or man? Feeling young or old? Some of you will have intense feelings, while others will have very mild feelings about life's movement. Different persons measure its meaning differently.

Second, transitions may sketch out growing edges, but they are also at times occasions for uprooting, separation anxieties, and particular losses. Indeed, the anxiety of grief is a strong candidate to be elected to "office" at these moments. The fact is that we really don't have to vote for it. Grief is a natural companion to separation, loss, or even the anticipation/apprehension of separation/loss. Grief has to do with our spiritual and emotional response to significant change. It just tends to show up to make itself known.

Young adults need the opportunity to understand and cope with their grief: exits—entrances; saying good-bye and hello; separation—belonging; giving up—taking on; and adjusting to—reorganizing. Stating that grief is life's unavoidable companion, Ramsay and Noorbergen outline phases and components of grief: shock, disorganization, searching behavior, emotional components (including pining, guilt, anger, shame, protest), letting go, resolution and acceptance, and reintegration.[14]

Oates shared a phase called the struggle between fantasy—as if it isn't happening—and reality—knowing that indeed something has changed.[15]

Some losses are inevitable. The point is that we grieve quite naturally over the *loss* of or change over anything/anyone important, crucial, necessary, valuable, or integrally linked to us. Jesus taught, "Blessed are they that mourn, for they shall be comforted" (Matthew 5:4, NIV).

Linus of the *Peanuts* comic strip said, "I can't live without that blanket. I can't face life unarmed." There will be "a good many" times when you will wonder why you are "flat," "blah," "down," "depressed," "feeling unarmed" about some of those transitions. As one young adult explained, "When I graduated from Georgia Tech and got that wonderfully exciting job in Philadelphia, I couldn't understand why I felt so immobilized for a good while." She was born, grew up, and educated entirely in Atlanta. That was her place—until now. Depression and anger normally seem to be "brothers or sisters" to losses and significant transitions. There will be days in which you would like to buy just a little more time before you really have to face some of these adult responsibilities.

A third factor involves quizzing the world, your place in it, your present way of doing things, the order of your values, and relationship to authority figures. "Perhaps I shouldn't be so compliant." "Maybe I need to seek out and find some new friends." "That preacher is so dogmatic." "Prayer?" "I do need to read more." "Why should I vote? I'm only one person." So the tussle goes on between appropriate, healthy self-assurance and the self-made attitude of "I don't need anybody. And furthermore what can you do for me anyway?"

Fourth, exploration or experimentation, sometimes in "far country" ways, may be an outcropping of one's questioning.[16] "There is no reason why I can't become a little more assertive in pursuing friendship with . . . (members of the opposite sex)." Levinson noted that the neglected parts of oneself tend to rise up to seek expression. Erickson called this a "moratorium," a "time off" or "time out" from "ordinary" role expectations to check out new roles, values, and beliefs. Illustrations of this vary from the high school student who takes a year or two off to work or enlist in the military before going on to college, to travel in Europe, or wherever. "I'm going to wait before I join that Sunday school class. I had to go to church all my life—every time the doors were open."

Young adults often comment about the pleasant memories they have of an attentive, caring adult who modeled mature faith, shared helpful experiences, and wise counsel. They may now lift out these as sturdy allies for entering young adulthood. Charles Shelton speaks of the "demoralization" pertinent to the adolescent experience that may carry over and tie into their young adulthood. "Demoralization," with its recurrent theme of "subjective incompetence," includes their confusion over goals, feelings of inadequacy, and subjective distress. More than likely, every late adolescent has difficulty feeling: (1) significant, (2) competent, and (3) powerful.[17]

Shelton calls the above the "SCP" method, as an aid for adult mentors caring for young adults.

- *Significance*—"Who is important to you?" What is it about those persons that makes them significant? And perhaps, "Who are you significant to?"
- *Competence*—"What do you enjoy doing?" Why do you like doing those "things?"
- *Power*—"Tell me about some decisions you've made in your life."[18]

If the adolescents are "bumfuzzled" or unable to talk about "SCP," explore with whom they might be significant, in what areas would they like to feel competent, and in what areas would they like to make nonfearful decisions. Hopefully, the young adult has already embraced the need of and actual fostering, affirming of "self-insight" with openness to God's communicated presence and Spirit; "value awareness," guided by worthy purposes and values; and "conscience formation," making maturing and healthy moral choices.[19]

## OUT ONE ERA AND INTO ANOTHER

Egan summarizes the developmental tasks of moving into and through adulthood:

1. Becoming competent
2. Achieving autonomy
3. Developing and implementing values
4. Forming an identity
5. Integrating sexuality into life
6. Making friends and developing intimacy
7. Loving and making a commitment to another person
8. Making initial job or career choices
9. Becoming an active community member and citizen
10. Learning how to use leisure time.[20]

Perhaps a new task for this generation is defining what is not good for them, and thus, what they need to stay away from.

Vivian McCoy, Colleen Ryan, and James Lichtenberg set out a different structure of stages from those of Egan. She calls the first developmental stage, roughly ages eighteen to twenty-two, "Leaving Home." The tasks of this stage are:

1. Breaking/accepting psychological ties
2. Choosing careers
3. Entering work
4. Handling peer relationships, such as whether peers are useful allies in understanding the hold of family
5. Managing time

6. Adjusting to life on one's own
7. Problem solving
8. Coping with stress as a companion to change.

The immediate next stage, "Becoming Adult," spans ages twenty-three to twenty-eight. These tasks continue the previous ones and also shift to:

1. Selecting a mate
2. Settling in work and even beginning a career "ladder"
3. Parenting and family formation
4. Emerging involvement in community
5. Wise consuming
6. Home ownership
7. Social interactions
8. Achieving autonomy and self-direction
9. Problem solving
10. Again coping with the stress of change.

The "Catch-30" stage, ages twenty-nine to thirty-eight, surfaces further variety:

1. Undergirding or searching for personal and meaningful values
2. Reappraising relationships
3. So-called progress or emergent success in career
4. Accepting and shifting with growing children
5. Roots and sense of permanency of home
6. Problem solving
7. Handling stress correlated to change.[21]

## Themes for Wholesome Living

### What Do I Do Well?

Most of us like to carry out our tasks with a nicely put "well, done!" Competence doesn't normally occur as a spectacular Hollywood production. It happens more down to earth, without a trumpet fanfare. Angela and Chris's sense of competence is the measurement of confidence they have in their ability to get things done in adequate amounts. Their actual competence refers to their ability to carry out these tasks.[22]

At this point, we can caringly help them identify some strengths as well as "soft spots." "Do I indeed see myself as a person who is capable of carrying through and getting things done?" "Do I have the resources needed—'stick-to-it-iveness,' inner strength, spiritual reserve—to accomplish goals I have set or dreamed for myself?" "In what areas of life do I especially handle myself well (or even more than adequate)?" "What areas would I like to be more effective in than I am?" "Am I willing to express my needs for assistance from others?"

The massive upsurge of computerization has complicated our perspective. The intrusion and enticement of chemical dependency is one of the greatest demonic challenges to the Christian's sense of mission and creative witness for Christ. As we minister with persons, keep in mind that competence includes such ingredients as the ability to endure reasonable degrees of frustration, subdue egocentrism/narcissism/ "the only me and no one else" impulse, and rightly accept/exercise authority. Set realistic goals that are not beyond your "stretch." Letting others dictate your goals may be a form of unrealistically high goal setting. On the other hand, setting goals that are unusually low or circular might not be beneficial because there is no striving or aspiring involved. An example of this is the young man who majored in physical education in college, not because he liked athletics, but because it was one of the easiest majors.

Self-worth has three important sources: God's creative image in us, conveyed as God's children taught by God's spirit; an inner source, the degree of effectiveness and nourishment of one's own activity; and an external source, the opinions of significant others about oneself. The first two are steadier and more dependable by far, than external sources. In fact, the apostle Paul wrote, "Such confidence as this is ours through Christ before God. . . . Our competence comes from God" (2 Corinthians 3:4-5, NIV).

In summary, competence refers to "how we do it" in these facets of life:

1. Physical/manual abilities, from coordination of body skills to living with handicaps

2. Social/emotional abilities in relating/expecting/reaching out decently, considerably, and faithfully to other persons, how this helps to determine and feeds into feelings of worth, to know what is called for in social situations, and social intelligence—when to respond appropriately
3. Self-management/caring skills
4. Interpersonal skills, including self-presentation, attending and active listening to others, responding to others, and challenging others ethically
5. The skills of small-group involvement, which at first seems "so easy."[23]

In actual experience it may be more difficult than it appears. "Are there small-group involvements in your life?" "What are the group's goals?" "Does the group encourage helpful conversations rather than negative complaints?" "Does this group promote competition or diversity within unity?" "What do you do well when you participate in it?"

The ministry of the church can be a facilitator or catalyst for matching persons in groups—Sunday school classes, interest or hobby groups, spiritual formation and equipping groups (i.e., prayer and Bible study types), friendship groups, and the Christian identity/ discipleship confronting his/her world.

Young adults want to believe they "belong" and are an integral part of the community of faith. "This is our church also." Jesus gave us a directive for the competency of loving each other (John 15:13-15). Hear some of the Apostle Paul's words as he focuses our confidence "in Christ." "I pray that out of his glorious riches he may *strengthen* you with power through his Spirit in your *inner being*, so that Christ may dwell in your hearts through faith. And I pray that you, being rooted and established in love, may have *power, together with* all the saints. . ." (Ephesians 3:16-18, NIV, author's italics). "Then we *will no longer be infants*, tossed back and forth by the waves, and blown here and there by every wind of teaching and by the cunning and craftiness of men in their deceitful scheming. Instead, speaking the truth in love, we will in all things *grow up* into him who is the Head, that is, Christ. From him the whole body joined and held together by every supporting ligament, *grows* and *builds* itself in love, as *each part does its work"* (Ephesians 4:14-16, NIV author's italics). (Study also Ephesians 4:22-29 and Philippians 2:4, 12-13, NIV.) Therefore, "Each one should test his own actions. . . . Let us not become weary in doing well, for at the proper time we will reap a harvest if we do not give up" (Galations 6:4,9, NIV).

## *Can I (We) Make It on My (Our) Own?*

Autonomy pertains to our capacity to attain reasonably safe self-sufficiency, but not at the expense of someone else. It is a challenge of moving toward mature, faithful interdependence. Four dimensions interface:

1. Our need for approval versus over-identifying with another's response;
2. Our ability to manage life independently, without continually or grudgingly seeking help from others;
3. The capacity for self-initiated planning, organizing, and problem solving; and
4. Awareness of how our needs relate to the needs of others, and thus the ability to integrate or to discern those needs.[24]

"Can I get things done all by myself?" "On a scale one to ten, with one representing overly dependent, ten representing overly independent, where do I find myself?" "Do I seem to be reasonably and fairly interdependent in my work, social life, church life?" "When I need help—whatever its normal form—do I find it awkward to ask for it?"

Autonomous persons are not hermits living on desert islands. They, in fact, recognize their need for others. They are respectful of the needs of others. Affirmations are needed. Yet, they themselves do not need continuous support, reassurance, and emotional "pats on the back." One young wife struggled with this: "It seems like no matter what I do, I'm watching to see if my husband and others really like it. Sometimes I get so worried about this that I fail to concentrate on what I'm supposed to be doing. I'm beginning to realize how this ties me up. I feel like a puff ball."

Be careful of *over*valuing the approval of others. "It'll wear your integrity out." Autonomous persons can certainly be married. If one's previous motto was "Do your own thing," then marriage deserves finding and maintaining balance between my/his needs with your/her needs. At one end of the continuum is the one who conveys, "I don't need you at all," and on the other end, "I need you desperately—now—quickly—forever present."

The following open statements are really some exercises to examine dependence, counterdependence, independence, and interdependence. Give one example of an experience in which you have been recently "nongrowthful" dependent. One college student shared, "I regret that I still take all my laundry home for my mom to wash." Share an example of dependence that enriched you! A wife wrote, "When I was put to bed to rest because of my anemic condition, my family waited on me. It was a welcomed relief."

Record a "nongrowthful" counterdependent experience. "I can't stand anyone in authority. No one's going to tell me what to do." Then illustrate a growth experience here. "I know I have the ability to write checks and keep a budget. I refuse to ask his help to untangle my procrastination."

Share an example of a way in which you displayed unproductive *independence*. "I decided to live in an apartment by myself during the fall semester. Boy, am I lonely!" On the other hand, record one beneficial to you. A new Christian in my Sunday school class confessed, "I realized that I don't have to drink at all to have friends." For interdependence, give a nonproductive example, followed by a successful one. "I'm not going to be wishy-washy anymore. We'll talk together about the decisions from now on."

The church's ministry might offer a chance for young adults to review and discuss goals individually, or in forums. Ministry in this sense becomes a "reality presenter." Pay attention to goals that:

1. Make sense to you and lead to accomplishments you value, which you are not ashamed of
2. Are concrete rather than blurry and general
3. Are in touch with the resources you have at hand
4. Motivate your willingness to put out
5. Have a time boundary for completion or renegotiation.[25]

*What Do I Believe "In"?*

What provides you with the basis for your ethical and spiritual development? Where do you "pledge your allegiances"? *You cannot commit to that which has no value to you.* The issue of moral development has attracted the attention of diverse responses. The *self*-centered layer, according to one view, asks, "Will the results of my behavior be pleasurable or painful for me?" The *other*-centered layer asks, "Will my behavior show loyalty to my significant affiliations—family, friends, Christ?" The *searching* stage asks, "How will my action come out in terms of this overarching standard?" The *committed* stage asks, "Am I morally clean by the criteria I have chosen?"

Pastoral strategy is interested in these kinds of concerns. "What are the things that are really valuable to me?" "Do I practice my values?" The Scriptures suggest, "Do not neglect your gift. . . . Be diligent in these matters; give yourself wholly to them so that everyone may see your progress. Watch your life and doctrine closely" (1 Timothy 4:14-16, NIV; also 2 Timothy 2:15, NIV). In summary it means: "Love the Lord your God with all your heart and with all your soul and with all your mind" (Matthew 22:33, NIV).

*Who in This World Am I?*

The decisive factor of *identity of selfhood* for the Christian is our encounter with Christ. "For we are his workmanship, created in Christ Jesus for good works, which God prepared beforehand that we should walk in them" (Ephesians 2:10, NIV). Identity is also the bridge between oneself and larger society. Out of the numerous possibilities, dreams, and hopes of childhood emerges your pattern/character style. The early childhood question, "Who will I be?" is now taking unique, urgent shape.

For the next few minutes begin with these personal exercises. "Do I have a good grasp of who I am and the direction I seem to be going in life?" "Am I ashamed of who I am and what I have done with life, or am I able to smile when all is said and done?" "Am I reasonably satisfied?" "Do I see myself as others see me?" "What/

who is the integrating center, the focus, that gives meaning (the theme) to my life?" "In what social contexts do I feel best about myself?" "In what social contexts do I feel 'smudged into the wallpaper'—a loss of distinctiveness?"

A combination of the theological themes of providence and awareness of the holy allows us to process pastorally where one's ultimate and transcendent meanings of life hold true. "Does the person perceive a divine purpose in his/her life?" "Does he have a sense of basic trust in the world?" "What is sacred to this individual?" "Is he suspicious of divine promises as they have been interpreted to him by a overpromising or rigidly demanding minister or church?" *"Does he believe God intends for him to experience well-being?"*[26]

Jesus, in his own young adulthood, was faced with the question of authentic and true identity, fully embracing the fact of "this is who I am" to the world. At his baptism John tried to deter him, but Jesus instructed, "Let it be so now, for thus it is fitting for us to fulfill all righteousness" (Matthew 3:15, RSV). A voice from heaven affirmed, "This is my beloved Son, with whom I am well pleased" (Matthew 4:15, 17, RSV). Later, he raised part of the identity question, "Who do you say I am?" ("Who am I to you?"). Peter answered, "You are the Christ" (Mark 8:27-30, RSV).

New insights are likely to happen if you spend a while completing this: "I am . . ." (or "I am one who . . .") and do this about ten times with a different response each time. Then design a presentation of your life mapping, "Let me tell you about where I've come from to get here!" These exercises can be used effectively in caring, friendly church groups to develop active listening, acceptance, and understanding of each other's history. The principle of James is a good communication vehicle. "Everyone should be quick to listen. . ." (James 1:19, NIV).

## *What Is the Place of Occupation/Work in My Life?*

"Just a housewife!" "Just a salesman!" Career or occupational choice is a process of decision making. It symbolizes more than a designed set of skills and functions. It means a way of life. "What do you do?" "Oh, really?" Unfortunately, there are tendencies to form snap judgments about people according to what they "do." Write brief responses to these open-ended statements:

- Choosing a career means for me _____.
- I've really considered/dreamed about the following vocations _____.
- If I had an ideal career where everything knitted together 'just right' for me, it would be _____.

"Expanding—narrowing—again, expanding—narrowing" is the pattern.[27] The expanding phase broadens the view of options or possibilities. The narrowing movement contracts or squeezes more tightly the focus and eliminates some options in favor of more promising or satisfying ones. "Where does college, or even post-graduate education fit in?" "Should I go now or wait?" "If we set the wedding for December, will that distract my partner from graduate exams?"

A self-inventory might include: "What are my feelings about the way I am preparing myself for a career?" "What are my predominant thoughts and feelings about my present position/work?" "What do I get out of my work?" "What is the workplace environment like?" "What typically goes on there?" "Where am I regarding my 'initial' career choice?" "Am I stuck?"

Pastoral strategy can serve as an enabler for action plans involving goals, resources toward achieving goals, and concrete programs, as well as being a "cheerleader." Vocational guidance, utilizing a variety of persons experienced in particular areas, opens dialogical participation, exploring, and understanding. Christian vocation is more than the work one does, or the career engaged in. It is helping neighbor and being ambassadors for Christ. Has God "called" you? If you are a Christian, the answer is a resounding yes. Learning the stewardship of our gifts wherever we work can be a channel of elevating work to a sense of vocation—"calling." "As each has received a gift, employ it for one another, as good stewards of God's varied grace" (1 Peter 4:10, NIV; see 1 Corinthians 4:2, NIV). In a broad sense, the word meaning could be put in the place of "calling." Thus, it might read, "the 'meaning' I give as a Christian to my work is. . . ." "Am I a cheerful participant in the scheme of God's creation?"

*The Gift of Sexuality Means to Me . . .*

"Who am I as a God-given sexual being?" Many Christian ethicists suggest that the way in which you see yourself as a sexual being is an important dimension of your overall identity.

This also influences how you relate to others as a sexual person. For example, if you see yourself only as an object of pleasure, then you may be exploited as a sexual pleasure object. Culture through the media, magazines, advertising, and now the Internet, especially, conveys many double messages and sex-role stereotypes. "What in the world does a bikini-clad beauty have to do with the value and efficiency of shaving cream, a new automobile, or toothpaste?" The beat goes on with that kind of absurdity and subliminal reduction-seduction. Most of us would find a new American car under $15,000 a very good buy, "sexy" or not.[28] What has happened is that commercialism and its myriad of marketplaces has taken away a holistic understanding of a kind of God-intended birthright. Sexuality had been reduced to sex, and sex reduced to the status of a commodity to be dispensed as reward for performance. This reductionism and purely recreational approach also dehumanizes the responsibility to receive, to claim, and to decide about the gift. The "fun sex" mentality is a reflection of a kind of incomplete, distorted valuing. The shabby moral reasoning for it seems to be, "If it feels good, it must be right." The question pastoral strategy needs to ask again and again is, "Is such sex really honest and received as a gift God gives?"

Assess these sentences carefully. "When I think of myself as a sexual being, I. . . ." (Write a paragraph or two.) "What I learned in my home (from parents) about sexuality and intimacy was. . . ." "The persons or social settings which introduced me to sexuality were: peers, classes in school, church groups, parents, or. . . ." "What did they teach me and what did I learn about the subject?" Furthermore, shifting gears to a correlated area, "What are the spiritual values that are significant to me that relate to my sexual life?" (List these!) "When I envision closeness with a person of the opposite sex, I tend to. . . ." "In terms of my sexuality, marriage for me means. . . ." "What are my expectations about 'what women should be' and 'what men should be?'" "How do these sex-role expectations affect my behavior?" "A good family life is. . . ." "A good marriage is. . . ." "A good friendship involves. . . ."

The church can provide dialogical conferences and forums to deal with society's voices and distortions. Marriage enrichment retreats/conferences, family/parent conferences/workshops, single adult "get-togethers" and study groups are just a few openings for these needs of information, biblical assessment and feedback.

There are many well-informed, trained pastoral counselors, pastors, church staff personnel, seminary teachers, teachers in Christian colleges, chaplains, and skilled laypersons, who are able to lead in the enriching and strengthening aspects of who we are. The pulpit is an apt place to proclaim good news for living. That is one place where we can be helped and guided to know theological underpinnings from the word of God. "Whatever happens, conduct yourselves in a manner worthy of the gospel of Christ" (Philippians 1:27, NIV). "Submit to one another out of reverence for Christ" (Ephesians 5:21, NIV). Therefore, "Be very careful, then, how you live—not as unwise but as wise . . ." (Ephesians 5:15, NIV).

## What Are My Closer Relationships Like?

If Angela and Chris have a healthy sense of who they are, they will begin to create stable personal relationships. Intimacy may include these elements: desiring the good for the other as much as you desire it for yourself; firm loyalty to the other; mutual support and availability; a shared view of the world; mutual self-disclosure; and shared, honest vulnerability. Intimacy does involve friendship. It is much more than mere sexual relationships.

Angela and Chris have experienced: strangers, acquaintances, friendships, and intimacies. At one end, they know strangers, persons who are really neither for or against them. They have many acquaintances that are known casually and informally. Sometimes these acquaintances become close friends. The intimate persons are the ones who know them deeply, perhaps even some of their inmost secrets. Not many of your relationships need to be like an open book to be read by just anyone.

Loneliness is the other side of friendship and intimacy. It is a very common experience in our culture and even in the sometimes crowded church. James Lynch in his book *The Broken Heart: The Medical Consequences of Loneliness* insists that persons who live alone are more susceptible than others to the likelihood of serious illness.[29]

Notice how both complicated and enriching our relationships can be, "How much of my day is absorbed in relating to other persons?" "Do I have several friends, and what kinds of closeness do I have with other persons?" "Where do these relationships generate—church, work, and so on?" "Is my life too crowded with people?" "Are there too few people in my life?" "Do I plan to get together with others who matter to me, or do I leave this to 'bump into' chances?" "What do I like and enjoy in other persons?" "Do I tend to need my friends more than they express need of me?" "How do others know I care for them?" "Do I take persons for granted?" "Do I allow others to care for me?" "Do I respect other persons?" "Am I willing to talk about myself appropriately with persons who convey closeness to me?" "Am I an active listener?" "What does being close to someone mean to me?" "How do you get in touch with them?" "Who am I particularly close to currently?" "Does closeness tend to arouse my anxiety and awkwardness?" "How do I encourage special persons to get closer to me?" "Do people see me as a distant, controlled person, or a balanced feeling person?" "Do they experience my anger or frustration more than my consideration and warmth?" "How do I handle my feelings when I'm with others?" "Especially, how do I respond when I perceive I'm being turned away?" "Have I ever been/felt rejected?" "Am I disappointed easily?" "Do I seem to want a fair amount of give-and-take in these relationships?" "For instance, what would I feel comfortable asking my friends?" "Am I a healthy compromiser, or an unbending controller?" "Do I expect to be treated as 'an equal,' and also to treat my friends 'as equals?'" "How do I get along generally in my school, work, church, family relationships?" "Do I permit others to be themselves?"[30]

If you will take a few moments, write out your own definition of intimacy. Jesus' intimacy and friendship with the Father becomes the foundation of our friendships and trustworthy intimacies as

Christians. "I and the Father are one" ("together"; see John 1:14-16, NIV). This issue enables us to share the power and nature of blessing with others in freedom.

### What Are My Deeper Interpersonal Commitments?

Vocational choice and marital choice are indeed two of the most significant life decisions. They become major determinants of your personality development and perhaps the style of life that you lead. Sometimes they are decided smoothly; other times with a good bit of flip-flopping. Yet they are complex matters. At this point, if you are married, these might be helpful inquiries. "What is our marriage like?" "What did I expect to be happening?" "What kind of relationship do I have to my parents now?" A triad of meaning enters the picture: love, marriage, family. When? The marriage ceremony gives permission to be responsibly adult. Marriage anxieties and adjustments need healing time. The church can be a suitable facilitator of enrichment, awakening hope, and constructive problem solving.

Some general reflection exercises on the nature and meaning of commitment would include: (1) "When I say that I am committed to another person, I mean. . . ." (2) Focus on a close, committed person to you and write down the qualities that accent its special meaning. (3) Pursue this. "What do you suppose happens for some relationships to take on commitment whereas others do not?"

Commitment is a pledge to do something, a binding to a course of action, and a meaning to stand alongside of and with the other (Romans 12:1). Commitment is to give oneself in trust. It gives a special flavoring to life. The Christian meaning of love involves responsiveness and commitment. Marriage is a visible, public, special commitment to responsibility before the creative Lord who "ordains" it. A committed young adult whether in friendship or in marriage does not live life in a "yes-but" style. The noncommitted person relies on a method of evasion that says yes and no at the same time. The committed person lets the yes be yes and the no be no. *Commitment is the antithesis of alienation.*[31]

There are some snag points that hinder wholehearted commitment: (1) a pervasive low sense of personal worth, (2) detachment from people, and (3) disenchantment with special causes, or centers of focus. Oates suggests that persons find it very hard to commit to that which they do not value. The church's ministry can illustrate and recall its great, long-standing heritage of care and the learned wisdom of its experience. We are made in the image of God. We are persons for whom Christ died. We belong to the Living Lord and to a community of faith who care. Hopefully out of this caring context will come a valuing of ourselves as we recognize we are valued by God. (See 2 Corinthians 1:17 to 22.)

## Do I Deserve Leisure Time?

In a workaholic, success-performance, highly productive, hurried world, we need to reclaim leisure as grounded in the doctrine of creation. The work-rest rhythm appears basically in the fact God himself labored six days and rested on the seventh (Genesis 2:1-3). At the heart of leisure is the issue of freedom. One's time can be used creatively or confusingly. The use of time is a factor in leisure also.

In a very fine article, Wayne Oates confronts the common assertion by couples, family members, and singles that you are unable to find time for yourselves and for each other. He surfaces some of those hidden obstacles that delay you from choosing to discover time.[32]

Pastoral strategy within the church can assess where it is adding to the problem of over-demand of time and not enough balance of being still, serendipitous, and life celebrators who enjoy. It may be that the church needs to help persons to know the times when they presume upon the grace and love of their marriages and families. Look for the thieves of your time! One of the major tasks of the church is to provide guidelines, methods, and means for the best use of free time by its members in terms of ministering to the whole person. Leisure is a gift from God for a purpose, whether to be used for vacations, sports, hobbies, or whatever. For the glory of God. Thus, these activities can become opportunities for deeper commitment to Christ and involvement in serving Him.

## Is My World Big Enough?

Explain what comes to mind when you hear the term citizen. "What are the social organizations and institutions that you feel will

have a necessary or important influence on you and/or your mar-
riage/family in the years to come?" "Is there personal investment in
the larger community beyond friends, work, marriage or family?"
"Is it high, medium, low?" "Do I have genuine community, civic,
political interests?" "Am I a detractor, impeding the group's goals/
work, a mere member, with nominal or little attention to what's
going on, an observer, a participant, contributor, or leader?"[33]

One response is a selective inattention or naïveté—"Everything
will be just fine"; and another is cynicism—"Everything is really
corrupt or hopeless, so why bother." Young adults in particular face
the sandtrap of this "either—or."

The Lord expects us to be effective, faithful Christians who know
how to be effective citizens with our eyes open, to live up to his
calling in terms of responsible citizenship (see Romans 12:21 to
13:1; 14:17-19; Matthew 22:21).

## SPIRITUALITY IN A CHANGING CULTURE

### The Desire for Safe Belonging

This generation of young adults do not like religious persons who
try to manipulate them with doctrinaire, unattainable, artificial slo-
gans. Personal relations and personally experienced testimony are
valuable and significant ways to communicate to them and "baby
busters," according to several who have studied this "culture." A
key biblical solution for keeping them in church is "making them
disciples." But the need to coach them to *develop a spiritual value
system* is a companion to discipleship ministry. There seems to be a
paradigm shift that recognizes humans as spiritual people, however,
that is defined or explained, in the midst of a continued information
revolution.

Many are learning to reverse an earlier drag-a-long theology that
imaged God as anything but one who wanted well-being and hopeful futures for us. There is a search for a liberating message that
says God longs for us to know in the depths of our being that God
loves us and God's acceptance of us is quite different from the way
we accept others and ourselves. As Joachim Jeremias, the New

Testament scholar helped us understand, God is our "Abba," our loving Father, an extraordinary "Dad," unlike any we have known, whether good ones or disgracefully neglecting ones. This Father knows us far better than we ever know ourselves. He wants us to have a more joyful, passionate fellowship with Him. One of the important questions about the young adults' spirituality was raised by Brennan Manning, *"Is an imposter robbing you of God's love?"*[34] What "things" are getting in the way of receiving God's goodness?

### *Spiritual Direction and Nurturance*

Where is our "Yes"? That is, where are our commitments? The following questions have been helpful in the spiritual formation of Angela and Chris. James Hyde, a longtime friend, shared these questions initially in a lecture at the Oates Institute.[35] They are paraphrased in the hope of creating conversation, direction, and nurturance.

1. What do we mean by spirituality? What is a spiritual person like when all is said and done? That is, what are his or her features (behaviorally, cognitively, emotionally)?
2. Does our spirituality speak *of* rather than *for* God?
3. Does our spirituality maintain a balance between solitude and community? The avoidance of community may center us on "self" only rather than the sacred.
4. Does it instruct and inspire us in the ways of God's love, and hold us accountable to each other in the presence of God's love, grace, and truth?
5. Does it comfort or disturb us in life and death themes? When we are most vulnerable to the crises of life, does our spirituality enhance our faith?
6. Does our spirituality make us aware of what one writer calls *"the practice of noticing"*—others in need, awareness of the stewardship of creation, and stewardship of our gifts to serve Him?
7. Does our spirituality direct us to the *practice of the presence?* Carlyle Marney told the story of a man who quietly entered a town in western New Mexico. The town was gripped by the

power of a group of bully cowboys. The man single-handedly organized the citizens and ran the bullies out of town. After he helped them establish law and order in their community, he moved on. The townspeople were so moved by his presence with them that they erected a huge sign at the entrance of the town. It read, "Wyatt Earp passe pore aqui," "Wyatt Earp passed by here." Are you aware of God's presence in the ordinariness of life?

Young adults need to learn that we are authentic, and not frauds, when we speak *of* God, rather than the grandiose task of speaking *for* God. Too often, we confuse God with our own inner voices, projecting those voices out as if it were God speaking. I recently heard a religious leader of a well-known Christian organization say that he and God are so close that when he speaks to his missionaries, it is the *same* as God speaking.

When we speak of God, we connect as one human being with another along life's journey, rather than having all the answers for our ambiguities. The spiritual position of speaking of God is the pilgrim-living-with-purpose, rather than the drifter, who has not stopped to figure out that God wants to have the significant focus in our lives. The belief in purposeful spirituality advocates that there is a basic human instinct for God, the sacred. It also illustrates our capacity to find the sacred, the extraordinary God, in the ordinary and mundane.

In her book *To Dance with God*, Gertrude Mueller Nelson[36] tells of sewing one afternoon and discarding scraps of fabric into a waste-basket. She noticed that Annika, her young daughter, was searching through the basket of scraps, selecting several long pieces with the brightest colors. She realized Annika had disappeared to the backyard into her own "world." When her mother found her, she was affixing the scraps to the top of a pole with huge stick wads of tape. Annika responded, "I'm making a banner for a procession. I need a procession so that God will come down and dance with us." With that, she slowly lifted the banner so it would catch and flutter in the wind. She slowly began to dance. Gertrude, like Annika, realized she had encountered the sacred, a sense of the Presence of God, in an ordinary experience.

How similar this encounter is to the experience of Moses and the burning bush. Ushered into the presence of God, Moses allowed himself to be embraced by the spirit of God. Herding sheep, out in nowhere, a barren, desert experience was transformed into hearing God's voice. Hopefully Angela and Chris are finding the truth that the spirit of God comes to us wherever we do our living—tending sheep, being single, being Mom or Dad, in the marketplace of jobs, in the kitchen, and so on—to comfort us in times of trouble and crisis; when we are powerless, helpless, lonely, or afraid. It comes when we get stuck in the "far country," wasting our inheritance, or have identified with the words of Mae West, an actress of an earlier day, "I used to be Snow White—but I drifted."

## Hide and Seek

When Angela and Chris were young, they loved to play Hide and Seek. Angela would say to her Dad, "I'm going to go hide, and you come find me." After a few minutes, her Dad would go searching, only to hear her giggle, "Come find me, Daddy, I'm behind the door." It is a spiritual truth that we all like to be "found," and not to continue to have to hide.

One way that young adults hide is pretending or believing we have to be perfect before God accepts us or as a condition for acceptance. Another way we hide from God's grace is allowing the dark side to say, "I am no good. I deserve to be forgotten, pushed aside, rejected." Henri Nouwen observed, *"Self-rejection is the greatest enemy of the spiritual life* because it contradicts the sacred voice that calls us the *'Beloved'*."[37]

Young adults have a spiritual task of learning to be gentle with themselves by experiencing the intimate, heartfelt compassion and friendship of Christ. To feel loved by God in a safe relationship. The words of Thomas Merton, the great spiritual guide that I was privileged to meet and converse with, are wise and applicable to any age. "Quit keeping score altogether and surrender yourself with all your sinfulness to God who sees neither the score nor the score-keeper but only his child redeemed by Christ."[38] Merton realistically reminded us that "Every one of us is shadowed by an illusory person: a false self."[39]

### Grace-Filled Spiritual Identity

If Angela and Chris seek an identity outside themselves, then they are lured by the accumulation of wealth, power, and ambition. When they draw life and meaning from any source other than as "Abba's Child," they are spiritually diminished, or even spiritually dead. The question of "Who are we?" comes alive when we respond, "We are ones loved by God-in-Christ."

Thus our spiritual identity is no longer masked by religiosity—doing religious work without awareness of the presence of God—or by religious rhetoric that deafens God's words of tenderness for us. Truly we may see the face of Christ and experience a smile rather than a smirk and frown. Brennan Manning summarizes the issue of needing to claim God's given grace. "Define yourself radically as one beloved by God. This is the true self. Every other identity is illusion."[40]

In Figure 4.1, find yourself on the tree in terms of where you are in your faith, commitment, and spiritual journey. What led you to identify and choose that place(s)?

## ADDITIONAL PRINCIPLES OF PASTORAL CARE

Muriel Jones, a well-known writer and friend, says that we live in a "laughter-starved" society. Lawrence Peter's prescription for humor therapy seems to offer some ready-made proverbs for ministering to this need for a different perspective:

1. Follow your doctor's advice.
2. Acquire positive expectations of health.
3. Laugh it up.[41]

Therefore, a paraphrase might read: "Follow the Lord's advice; acquire positive expectations of spiritual well-being; and enjoy." If only life happened in that glib manner and we had that kind of proverbial influence over people! The metaphor from a poster I saw once might be a better starting place. "Walking isn't a lost art—one must, by some means, get to the garage." There is no one way to care for young adults. They may be single, married, or formerly

FIGURE 4.1. An Exercise for Reflection

married. However, we will try walking, getting to the garage, and other means to attempt to get in touch with them.

## *Learning the Laughter of Faith*

Since so much voicing in our world dwells on the critical, the fearful, the sad, and the distorted, learning how to enhance and to harness our God-given creative powers to joy in life is an important task. Jonathan Swift, English satirist of the eighteenth century, summarized health care as: "The best doctors in the world are Dr. Diet, Dr. Quiet, and Dr. Merryman," seems appropriate. Humor as a first cousin of joy is part of our reserve to handle our faith.

Albert Schweitzer once wrote that "each patient carries his own doctor inside him." Take some of that self-defeating energy and turn it to wellness. Laughter as a kind of spiritual doctor inside you brings about beneficial physiological results as well as spiritual energy to relieve stress, alleviate pain, and wipe out anger (compare, James 1:19-20; Ephesians 4:20, 26-32). Laughter exercises the lungs, stimulates the circulatory system, and uses all of our major organ systems. It reduces muscle tension. Moreover, a sense or attitude of humor—not allowing things to get us down, the ability to see through our pretensions, the capacity for hope and endurance, and revising inflated expectations—is related to a positive, enriching attitude and the will to live.

Indeed, a sense of humor enlarges our capacity to relax in order to renew strength and vision, to see the inconsistencies in our behavior, to resolve problems, to create our own mirth, to laugh at illness and crisis, and to communicate effectively. Peter's prescription for growing a sense of humor includes the following:

1. Adopt an attitude of playfulness—it is OK to be silly at times, so give yourself healthy permission.
2. Think funny.
3. Laugh at yourself—not in derision, but in acceptance of the fact "I am unfinished. Here's a recent example."
4. Take yourself "lightly."[42]

Unfortunately some have a view that religion and humor do not mix because laughter is linked with worldliness and nonseriousness. But listen to scripture. "The morning stars sang together, and all the sons of God shouted for joy" (Job 38:7, NIV). Spiritual life in Christ is an amazing, wondrous gift to be enjoyed. Perhaps George Buttrick with a wink in his eye is on track, "No somber God could ever have made a bullfrog or a giraffe."[43] I once had a student who responded to a discussion on the providential care of God by asking, "Does God ever smile for you—at you?"

The Gospel accounts of the birth of Jesus have joy (and rejoicing) as their common theme. Furthermore, "the Word became flesh and dwelt among us" (John 1:14, NIV) is the central affirmation of the New Testament. God has come close to us not as an enemy but as a savior and friend (John 15:15). His message is redeeming, reconciling love. In a sense, we can laugh from relief. The laugh is one of amazement, delight, disbelief that he really does love us, and a faith that takes over with assurance. How else can we respond but to give back our shouts of joy and to enjoy his created things? Jesus said, prior to the Passion events, "Be of good cheer, I have over-come the world" (John 16:33, NIV).

### *Getting in Touch with Your Gift*

Chris and Angela as individuals—as young adults—are theologically a gift from God. Understanding their personhood as a gift is foundational to their Christian life. "How do they receive gifts?" "Are they thankful?" Life is not something that we create out of nothing. We really did not earn it. It is a gift through the processes and mystery of life given to our parents. Thurl Ravenscroft, the longtime voice character of Tony the Tiger on the Kellogg's ad for Frosted Flakes cereal, once visited the college campus where I was a dean and chaplain. He was sharing the fact that he had major surgery that brought unexpected news many years ago. As he lay in his hospital bed wondering what was coming next, he realized anew that his life was really a gift from God. He explored the options available in receiving a gift, such as: apathy, acting as if God wasn't involved in life; cynicism, self-madeness, not feeling responsible to or needing anyone else; or finally thanksgiving, recognizing and claiming the gift. The proper response to a gift is indeed "thanks." There has never been anybody before us or anybody who will come after us who is exactly like us. My life as a gift? In Christ, life and life anew is an inexpressible gift, given by grace, not earned (Ephesians 2:7-10).

The self-made concept, which the Pharisees of Jesus' day seemed to embody, is one that says, "You owe me! And what can you do for me? It is not, 'What can I give you?' The Pharisees have arrived, so don't bother me!" Someone has suggested that the self-made person is one who really does not know how to say thanks or at least functions out of an inability or reluctance to say it to those who have supported, taught, prayed for, befriended, guided, and stood by them.

Learning to reinforce our ability to say thanks to God for our lives is part of the maturing wisdom of the young adult. I have learned that a thankful person is a hopeful person. Thankful people tend to "esteem" their worth as children of God. Young adult, take hold of your gift with thanks—living. (See Figure 4.2 for an overview of young adult tasks, pastoral strategies, and desired implementations.)

FIGURE 4.2. Overview of a Young Adult's Developmental Tasks and Pastoral Strategies[44]

| Developmental Layer | Pastoral Strategy/ Program | Implementation Desired |
|---|---|---|
| "Leaving Home" 18-22 | 1. Educational/career/ vocational guidance and information, clarification/reorganizing levels via questionnaires/conferences<br>2. Personal growth and enrichment, building workshops/"taking hold of your gift" theme<br>3. Interpersonal-communication skills/groups<br>4. Homemaking/parenting workshops<br>5. Living by oneself/ creative singles workshops<br>6. Time management/ using gifts in ministry<br>7. Stress without distress<br>8. Life situation Bible study<br>9. Preparation/ readiness for marriage/ conferences | 1. Well-fitting career decisions<br>2. Claiming one's gift of life<br>3. Effective/informed social interacter, responder/consumer<br>4. Healthy home life<br>5. Worthy single life<br>6. Crisis/problem solver<br>7. Balanced and diverse stress management<br>8. Learning to delay gratification rather than demanding instant gratification<br>9. Prayer/meditative lifestyle<br>10. Learning to say thanks (Colossians 3:15-16) |

| Developmental Layer | Pastoral Strategy/ Program | Implementation Desired |
|---|---|---|
| "Becoming an Adult" 23-28<br><br>(Some overlap of prior layer) | 1. Neo-married/ marriage retreats/ groups<br>2. Parenting/child's esteem conferences<br>3. Owning/buying a home<br>4. Living as a single/ formerly married conferences<br>5. Creative problem solving/communica- tion<br>6. Volunteer dynamics/ leadership roles and "causes"<br>7. Coping with stress | 1. Effective growing marriages<br>2. Occupational satisfaction<br>3. Healthy, consistent parenting<br>4. Informed citizen<br>5. Well-being in home life<br>6. Confidence in where one is as a single<br>7. Enhancing problem- solving abilities<br>8. Personal growth in handling transitional stress |
| "Catch 30"<br><br>(The gap between leaving home and here begins to shape out) | 1. Owning what is important/clarifying values/expectations<br>2. Marriage counseling/ enrichment groups/ communication assessment workshops<br>3. Parent-child concerns<br>4. Consumer interests/ financial planning<br>5. Crisis groups—grief, formerly married, etc.<br>6. Problem solving negotiations<br>7. Stress management | 1. Examining/owning one's commitments/ "importances"<br>2. Faithful personal relationships<br>3. Sense of achievement/ competence in one's work<br>4. Growth beneficial to parent-child interactions<br>5. Responsible con- sumer behavior<br>6. Appropriate problem solving/conflict negotiation<br>7. Personal growth in coping with life's changes |

## NOTES

1. Bouwsma, William J. "Christian Adulthood," in *Adulthood*, Ed. Erik Erikson. New York: W.W. Norton and Co., 1978, pp. 81-85.

2. Lidz, Theodore. *The Person*. New York: Basic Books, Inc., 1968, p. 362.

3. Ibid.

4. Satir, Virginia. *Peoplemaking*. Palo Alto, CA: Science and Behavior Books, Inc., 1972, p. 3.

5. Ibid., pp. xi, 3-6.

6. Ibid., pp. 4-5, 9-19.

7. Egan, Gerard and Michael A. Cowan. *Moving Into Adulthood: Knowledge and Skills for Effective Living*. Monterey, CA: Brooks/Cole Publishing Co., 1980, pp. 1-11, for a discussion of the challenges facing the young adult. *See also* Egan, Gerard. *You and Me: The Skills of Communicating and Relating to Others*. Monterey, CA: Brooks/Cole, 1977.

8. Levinson, Daniel J. *The Seasons of a Man's Life*. New York: Alfred A. Knopf, Inc., 1978, p. 73.

9. Coleman, Lucien E. Jr. *Understanding Today's Adults*. Nashville: Convention Press, 1982, p. 91.

10. Egan and Cowan, pp. 11-17.

11. Levinson, pp. 90-111.

12. Sheehy, Gail. *Passages: Predictable Crises of Adult Life*. New York: E.P. Dutton and Co., Inc., 1976, pp. 204-240.

13. Egan and Cowan, p. 21.

14. Ramsay, Ronald W. and Rene Noorbergen. *Living with Loss*. New York: William Morrow and Co., Inc., 1981, pp. 66-75.

15. Oates, Wayne. *Your Particular Grief*. Philadelphia: The Westminster Press, 1981, p. 103.

16. Egan and Cowan, pp. 27-29.

17. Shelton, Charles M. *Pastoral Counseling with Adolescents and Young Adults*. New York: Crossroad, 1995, pp. 17-18.

18. Ibid., p. 18.

19. Ibid., pp. 18-26.

20. Egan and Cowan, p. 32.

21. McCoy, Vivian Rogers, Colleen Ryan, and James W. Lichtenberg. *The Adult Life Cycle: Training Manual and Reader*. Lawrence, KS: The University of Kansas, 1978, p. 229. *See* Appendix I for an adaptation of these tasks, program outcomes sought to pastoral strategy.

22. These themes, starting with competence, are derived from Egan and Cowan and will be used throughout to blend with pastoral care approaches.

23. Egan and Cowan, p. 51f.

24. Ibid.

25. Ibid., pp. 82-119.

26. Pruyser, Paul. *The Minister As Diagnostician*. Philadelphia: The Westminster Press, 1976, pp. 62-67.

27. Egan and Cowan, pp. 236-253.

28. Ibid., pp. 154-174.

29. Lynch, James. *The Broken Heart: The Medical Consequences of Loneliness*. New York: Basic Books, 1979, p. 4.

30. Ibid., pp. 185-212.

31. Oates, Wayne. *The Psychology of Religion*. Waco: Word Books Publishers, 1973, pp. 222-225.

32. Oates, Wayne. "The Psychosocial Dynamics of Family Living," *Review and Expositor*, 75:1 (Winter 1978), pp. 67-74.

33. Egan and Cowan, p. 259.

34. Manning, Brennan. *Abba's Child: The Cry of the Heart for Intimate Belonging*. Colorado Springs, CO: Navpress, 1994, pp. 29-45.

35. Hyde, James. "Spiritual Direction in the Changing Culture." *The Bulletin of the Wayne Oates Institute*, 1998, pp. 3-4.

36. Ibid., p. 3.

37. Nouwen, Henri. *Life of the Beloved*. New York: Crossroad, 1992, p. 21.

38. Finley, James. *Merton's Palace of Nowhere*. Notre Dame, IN: Ave Maria Press, 1978, p. 53.

39. Ibid., p. 34.

40. Manning, p. 59.

41. Peter, Lawrence J. *The Laughter Prescription*. New York: Ballantine Books, 1982, p. 11.

42. Ibid., p. 193.

43. Buttrick, George. *Sermons Preached in a University Church*. New York: Abingdon Press, 1959, p. 52.

44. McCoy, Vivian Rogers, Colleen Ryan, and James W. Lichtenberg, pp. 229f.

## ANNOTATED BIBLIOGRAPHY

Arnold, William V. and Margaret Anne Fohl. *When You Are Alone*. Louisville: Westminster/John Knox Press, 1990.

> Assesses the positive values of solitude as well as the negative problems of loneliness. Underscores the power and intensity of various experiences of being alone.

Barna, George. *The Second Coming of the Church*. Nashville: Word Publishing, 1998.

> Pleads for God's people to stop dabbling in region and grow in spiritual maturity. Warns that the church is on the verge of losing its "platform" if it does not make meaningful changes.

Clinebell, Howard, J. *Anchoring Your Well-Being: Christian Wholeness in a Fractured World*. Nashville: Upper Room Books, 1997.

> Identifies seven areas as a way to integrate biblical insights and our human condition, such as spiritual well-being, mental well-being, physical well-being, relational well-being, crisis and loss well-being, work and play well-being, and environmental well-being.

Clinebell, Howard, J. *Growth Counseling for Marriage Enrichment: Pre-Marriage and the Early Years*. Philadelphia: Fortress Press, 1975.

> Utilized what he calls "the intentional marriage method" for making good marriages even better.

Grenz, Stanley J. *A Primer on Postmodernism*. Grand Rapids: William B. Eerdmans Publishing Company, 1996.

> Charts the postmodern landscape. A helpful introduction to the various cultural expressions, including TV, art, and so forth, that make up postmodernism.

Hoyt, Karen. *The New Age Rage*. Old Tappan, NJ: Fleming H. Revell Company, 1987.

> Contrasts New Age worldviews with biblical worldviews by assessing New Age as spiritual counterfeits.

Leman, Kevin. *The Birth Order Book: Why Are You the Way You Are?* New York: Dell Publishing, 1985.

> One's birth order powerfully influences what kind of person you are, who you marry, the job you choose, the kind of parent you will be.

Okimoto, Jean Davis and Phyllis Jackson Stegall. *Boomerang Kids*. Boston: Little, Brown and Company, 1987.

> A valuable resource for families facing the challenges of an adult child's return home, whatever the reason—divorce, loss of job, and so on.

Parrott, Les and Leslie Parrott. *Becoming Soul Mates: Cultivating Spiritual Intimacy in the Early Years of Marriage*. Grand Rapids: Zondervan Publishing House, 1995.

> A road map for cultivating rich spiritual intimacy in your relationship based on fifty-two practical devotions.

Parrott, Les and Leslie Parrott. *The Marriage Mentor Manual*. Grand Rapids: Zondervan Publishing House, 1995.

> A help for newlywed couples to stay married by strengthening their relationship.

Chapter 5

# The Middle Years: Getting It Together

George H. Gaston III

The journey of an individual's life moves into its midstages generally between the ages of thirty-five and forty. Persons who arrive at this juncture embark on life's potentially longest season of personal development. Those individuals who live to senior adulthood will spend approximately twenty to twenty-five years in the midranges of life. The numerous challenges found in midlife are best described as complex opportunities calling for determination and persevering hope.

The middle years, for the most part, really are not times for settling down. Anyone who paints the canvas of midlife as a season simply for enjoying the fruits of one's labor, misses the dynamism of these years. Even those middle-age persons who have an abundance of life's comforts and securities are faced with the internal and external complexities of life. The middle years truly are active years for pulling together the fuller meaning and purpose of one's life. In preparation for the senior years, each person has much developmental work to accomplish in the middle.

Of course, individuals do not arrive at this new stage of maturity as empty vessels or blank tablets. They are the products of over thirty-five years of living. The life strengths and weaknesses they have gained through interaction with their family experience, culture, education, friendships, crises, vocation, and religion will influence their capacity for traveling through the middle years. Some will approach this time as overly wounded pilgrims, ill-equipped for the difficulties to be faced. Lacking a dynamic sense of personal strength, they will stumble and fall over the threats to their finitude.

On the other hand, those who have been immersed in relationships of love and appropriate security will respond with a spirit of faith and hope, even though at times they will stumble. This reality, coupled with the uniqueness of each person, dictates that every individual will approach midlife quite differently.

In recent years, the literature on midlife developmental issues has expanded rapidly. Scores of books that describe and diagnose solutions for the dilemmas of midlife fill the shelves of bookstores and libraries. As members of the baby-boom generation have journeyed through midlife, they have produced an impressive body of literature on the realities of middle age. Groundbreaking works such as Daniel J. Levinson's *The Seasons of a Man's Life* and the popular *Passages: Predictable Crises of Adult Life* by Gail Sheehy have helped to pave the way for the literary explosion on median adulthood.[1] One of the earliest volumes to address the midlife issues from the vantage point of the Christian faith was Reuel L. Howe's *The Creative Years: A Mature Faith for Adult Life.*[2] Sadly, since Howe's groundbreaking book, literature produced by the faith community has been limited.

Those of us who minister to human need through the church should look carefully into such research for clues and directional signals on caring for the middle-age person. The gap existing in the church's understanding of and ministry to the midlifers seems obvious. We are, no doubt, perplexed by the challenges and traumas that occur in the lives of middle-age adults, but have little innovative and helpful ministry for these persons. We focus our energy on the young who are preparing for life and sometimes forget that life is a continual process of preparation. Hopefully, this chapter will add to the discussion on ministry among persons between the ages of thirty-five and sixty, as we explore what it means to be an adult in midlife.

## DEVELOPMENTAL THEORISTS

Scholars who have studied and sought to describe the midlife experience have labeled the central growth challenge of this time frame in a variety of ways. Look closely, however, and you will discover a common theme that is in all of their midlife descriptions.

Consistently, the developmental challenge of midlife that is presented as the key growth issue mirrors the biblical call to faith. Their writings do not always discuss God or the gospel, but they do delineate an unavoidable human questing during the middle years for the meaning of life and ways to make life a richer experience.

## L. J. Sherrill

A pioneer in the effort to correlate theology and psychology, theologian Lewis Joseph Sherrill wrote an intriguing volume in 1951 titled *The Struggle of the Soul.* He described a scheme of life that involved five major phases: childhood, adolescence, young adulthood, middle adulthood, and the senior-adult experience. Sherrill's book was an early contributor to the process of teaching young seminarians the developmental nature of life. The book challenged them to trace the human life of faith from childhood to old age.

Sherrill explored five struggles that coincided with the stages of life: becoming an individual; become independent from parents; finding one's basic identifications in life; achieving a mature view of life and the universe; and developing a simplified view of life so that the soul may proceed on to its chosen destiny. The description of a midlife struggle, achieving a mature view of life and the universe, was set forth as each person's natural quest to find life's meaning and to live for values that satisfy. Sherrill described the process of arriving at such a view of life and universe as the development of a life philosophy that helps one to discover the essence of life. He wrote:

> In this matter of a philosophy of life it is quite possible that we are dealing with an activity of the mind which is exactly as instinctual as growth itself. For the making of a philosophy of life is the self striving to relate, not to parts, but to the whole. It is striving to relate, not now merely to persons, or things, or to society and the flux of human events, or the world of adult life; but rather to the totality of all that has been, or is now, or ever shall be.[3]

Sherrill was correct in noting that not all persons develop a philosophy of life that is clearly directed toward self-giving. Even so, the struggle to understand the nature and purpose of life takes place in adults during midlife. Hopefully, they come to see the truly important things that help life open up into the fullness that existence holds for all who will obediently trust and journey onward in flexibility, integrity, and relationship.

### Daniel J. Levinson

Daniel J. Levinson projected a theory of adult development for males that is rooted in psychological research and terminology. In *The Seasons of a Man's Life,* Levinson identifies the developmental work of midlife transition as that of questioning life's structure. For some, the transition is quite severe, causing the unfolding of what Levinson labels a midlife crisis. As a man moves through his transition (or crisis), he must come to terms with the values and processes of his life. In the final analysis of things, the person must alter either his value system, the approach to his work, the structure and approach to his family life, or all of these. In effect, a man that is moving through midlife is rebuilding his life. He asks himself such questions: "What have I done with my life?" "What do I really give to and receive from my spouse, children, work, friends, community, and self?" "What is it I truly want from myself and others?"[4]

Like Sherrill, Levinson seems to suggest that the midlife transition struggle is an expected product of chronological aging. As persons become older, they automatically move through the inevitable transitions of existence. Levinson sets out the midlife developmental struggle in terms of meaning and approach to life. He believes persons are creatures who arrive at the midpoint asking questions about the purpose of existence. Once this struggle has begun to be resolved, the person can go on to live out the fullness of the middle years and beyond.

### Gail Sheehy

Based in part upon the work of Levinson, Gail Sheehy, in her widely read *Passages: Predictable Crises of Adult Life,* identifies the middle-age development issue as that of growing simultaneously on three basic adult frontiers: work, relationships to significant others, and the relationship to oneself. Her thesis emphasized the importance of persons growing toward authenticity. She declared:

> It is for each of us to find a course that is valid by our own reckoning. And for each of us there is the opportunity to emerge reborn, authentically unique, with an enlarged capacity to love ourselves and embrace others.[5]

Sheehy sees the middle thirties as being the literal midpoint of life, a time, "if we let ourselves," to have a "full-out authenticity crisis."[6]

The work that Sheehy has done fits nicely beside that of both Sherrill and Levinson. She, too, understands persons to be dealing with the meaning of all things, attempting to find a mature, acceptable approach to living as an adult. The midlife individual begins to have a changing sense of time, a growing desire truly to be alive, a reappraisal of self and others, and a reframing of life's priorities.

## Erik Erikson

One of the most important theorists to wrestle with the nature of midlife is Erik Erikson. Erikson's eight-stage psychosocial framework on the development of man is renowned. He focused the midlife adult development crisis around two polarities: generativity and stagnation or self-absorption. The middle-age person seeks to develop a sense of generativity without giving over to the debilitating process of stagnation and self-absorption. For Erikson, this issue is ethical in nature. He suggested that the matter is not so much an item related to chronological development as it is related to the ethical virtue of care. As an individual arrives at a point in life when relationships, children, vocation, and values have been established, the person must then determine if she or he will care for that which has been generated. *Generativity,* a word coined by Erikson, means to care about, and for, the future by investing something of yourself in nurturing those persons, causes, and values that will go on after you and will help make the planet a better place for the offspring of the human family. Fundamentally, generativity has to do with establishing and growing the next generation of humanity.

Erikson emphasized the necessity of getting under the load of life. The middle-age adult who refuses this challenge is the person who slips into the stagnation of self-absorption. The truth is, each midlifer is caught somewhere between generativity and stagnation. Some arenas of life will be filled with generativity, others will know the pollution of stagnant waters. The consistent challenge is to move toward generativity.

### The Midlife Issue: A Summary

Basically, the issue confronting the person in midlife is that of deciding to live a productive human life, in spite of the inevitable life changes that confront the person. In particular, the struggle is one of determining who one is, what one needs to be doing in life, and where one wants to establish one's life. It is a concern brought on by the passing of years and the arrival of the person at a responsible level of being. Somewhere at age thirty or forty, when a person has put down some roots, tasted a measure of achievement, and begun to realize the unreachable parts of life, the midlife struggle unfolds in earnest. The person begins to struggle to attain a meaningful, and hopefully mature, life philosophy.

Theologically speaking, all of this is born of the Holy Spirit. It is the spirit who meets us all along the road of life and calls us onward to the next plateau of being. God is at work in the middle-aged adult, asking for an evaluation of one's priorities and life goals. No matter that a person does not acknowledge God's presence. The calling to faith and life is from Beyond. The temptation to stagnate and become self-absorbed dates back to the Garden of Eden and humankind's fall. Those who will hear God's voice and move forward to live with authenticity, generativity, and responsibility will discover the full reward of life's deepest joy.

As one who is called to minister among middle-age sojourners, you must be alert to the overarching developmental concern at the "midpoint" in life. Learn to see midlifers as those who are going through a real identity crisis. View them as philosophers who are asking questions that go to the core of life. Your temptation will be to miss the big issue through being snared in the web of smaller issues composing the day-to-day existence of the midlifer. You will want to equip yourself as a helper to guide them through the unavoidable maze of challenges and struggles they confront on their way to a more mature philosophy of life.

## TEMPTATIONS TO STAGNATION: ISSUES ALONG THE WAY

What are the life issues that confront midlife adults and tempt them toward stagnation? What causes them to begin questioning life and evaluating the way they have lived it? Now that the big picture has been sketched, attention will be given to the particular issues that give rise to the philosophical dilemma of the middle-adult experience. An understanding of these consistent hurdles looming in the middle of the race is essential. They are the concrete opportunities by which the middle-aged individual will either develop generativity or stagnation.

### Bodily Processes

At some point in a person's late twenties, the body ceases to wax and starts to wane. Time takes its toll on the human body. Bodies that once seemed indestructible begin to show signs of obvious changes and unavoidable decline associated with older adulthood. As a result, persons begin to develop a subtle sensitivity and decreasing confidence in the ability of their bodies to perform as they used to. Wrinkling and sagging skin, graying and/or receding hair, stiff joints, enlarging hips and stomachs, and weakening, flabby muscles all begin to produce anxiety within the heart of an adult.

The fact that humans are viewed biblically as unified beings (not to be divided into unrelated parts such as body, mind, and soul) helps one to understand the reason bodily changes are often traumatic to individuals. The body is an expression, in part, of who a person is. Identity is bound up in physical appearance. Hence, when the body begins to move toward an obvious pattern of decline, the person begins to face the finitude of humanity. Such awareness can be most threatening. Increased efforts to keep the body young are often employed. Many persons cope with bodily changes through jesting. A recent cartoon quipped: "As I approach middle age, I'm developing a bad problem—my shirts and I taper in different directions." Comedian Bob Hope is attributed with having cleverly defined middleage as that time of life "when your age starts to show around your middle."[7] How good it is to see humor in our humanity! Nonetheless, even the jokes we tell speak of our anxiety about aging. Laughter is one way of easing some of the tension.

In America, the process of aging is complicated by a culture that worships physical beauty and youth. Oriental cultures conversely are known for their reverential treatment of the mature. The American advertising industry flaunts the qualities of youth and promotes products that purport to slow the aging process. Athletes and entertainers seem to be the folk heroes of our day. Many middle-age adults, unable to prevent their bodies from showing age, suffer from a real decline in self-appreciation. Thus, midlife persons often try to find renewal through becoming workaholics or frenzied physical exercise fanatics, or through venturing into a sea of irresponsible living as they search for affirmation. Has the church added to this problem by elevating the virtues of strength, beauty, and youth over those of maturity, experience, and wisdom?

### *Goals of Life*

A second painful issue midlife adults must encounter is the emotional struggle that accompanies the inevitable evaluation of the life goals established in younger years. Setting goals for life seems to be a natural phenomenon among humans.

Not all of our goals are established in openness or formulated intentionally. Even so, in some fashion all persons will formulate the images and dreams for successful living. These goals will guide the direction and intensity of a person's life. Goals may often be traced to childhood. Parents may subtly project their unfulfilled dreams upon their children. For instance, the nebulous goal of being wealthy could stem from a family that struggles through many rough years "trying to make ends meet." A host of the objectives that adolescents and young adults set for themselves can be rooted in the vague desires and "vows" of childhood.

Not all of life's visions are traceable to fuzzy beginnings. Persons are constantly responding to the various crises of human development through making decisions about their personal identity, and through setting intentional goals for the direction of their lives. Life priorities also can stem from one's spiritual and religious encounters, educational processes, and the awareness of needs that are present in society.

What does this issue have to do with midlife? By the time a person reaches middle age, many of life's pursuits have been accomplished and many are still unfulfilled (and perhaps never will be realized). Both realities can prove perplexing. A thirty-six-year-old dentist brags and laments: "I've already accomplished everything I set out to do. Where do I go from here?" A forty-year-old parent of four children begins to understand that his or her offspring aren't going to become the "successful" persons he or she had dreamed them to be, and the parent feels like a failure. Midlifers who decide to change careers, go back to school, or move to another place often do so in an effort to relieve the internal tensions that come with the struggle over life's goals.

The middle years are a time for celebration and also for feeling the pangs of failure and guilt over unrealized goals. Likewise, it is an occasion for feeling lost at the top with no further mountains to be climbed. Hopefully, middle age can be one of the most creative times of life. As one faces and accepts life's limitations, passing through the process described by Sheehy as the "de-illusionment of our dreams," one is able to set more realistic goals.[8] The successful feelings of accomplishment of sought-after dreams should be the fuel that sets persons on their way toward different and new horizons. Many who grow stagnant in midlife do so for lack of guidance beyond guilt, frustration, or realized success. Surely the church and its ministers of concern will want to serve as agents who equip and guide persons on their way to the City of Abraham's faith.

## *Letting Go of Responsibilities*

Another potentially threatening change for the middle-age individual, having enjoyed some measure of responsibility and power, is the ascent of humanity's next generation. Not long after a person begins to feel comfortable with the use of power, there comes the realization that others are standing nearby asking for the privilege of sharing the power. Such awareness can be quite disconcerting. It reminds midlifers that they are aging. "Where has the time gone?"

Only "yesterday" the one in the middle was making the decisions necessary to take hold of power. And now, someone younger wants the middle-aged adult to release and share a portion of the power—or perhaps give it up all together.

An inevitable struggle is set in motion, as a person's perceived power base is threatened. Human beings don't give up their territory with ease. Created to have dominion and to subdue the earth, persons doggedly stake out their areas of responsibility. The powerful deception of our sinful nature causes us to desire ownership and ultimate control. We lose sight of the God-given reality that life is to be lived as stewards (overseers) of the process and not despots. Life, however, has a way of reminding us about that stewardship. As a result, midlife persons quite often find themselves struggling to share their responsibilities and power.

Pastors will sense this real battle in the lives of their middle-aged parishioners as they take note of the marked increase apathy and withdrawal. Their countenance often cries out, "What's the use!" Consistently, the struggle can be seen in the way midlifers begin to compete for their role of leadership in the church. Anger will be on the increase with some. They may determine to hold onto things the way they've "always" been. Change becomes increasingly difficult. At times, midlife people tend to dig a frontline trench and hold off the onslaught of the aggressor. Unless this mentality is addressed in the church, adults will slip into the reality of deep stagnation and self-absorption. They must be helped to join hands with the wide generations of life. They stand in the middle of life, and in such a position are indispensable links between the generations of mankind.

## Changing Relationship Structures

By the time a person reaches middle age, a web of relationships has been established. These are vitally important contacts in which individuals are nurtured. Some of their relationships stretch back to the cradle. Others are recent additions to the person's support structure. As the person has dared to interact with fellow sojourners, identity and life's purpose have come into focus. The stability of these relationships is crucial for the person's well-being and sense of hope for life. Because this is true, one of the most trying parts of midlife is found in the multiple changes that happen in the support structure of every median adult. Some midlife theorists believe the most difficult part of living through these years is found in the instability of relationships. Every relationship that has helped to form the person will be tested, altered, or permanently lost during the years of middle adulthood.

## Aging Parents

One of the most demanding changing relationships for the middle-age adult is their relationship with their aging parents. Parents who have lived to be senior adults present their midlife children with increased life-support needs. Not only must midlife persons care for their own immediate families, but they must also begin now to have an expanded role in the care and attention of their parents. The extent of the care varies. Monetary provisions, shared dwellings, daily visits, occasional contacts, and ongoing advocacy on their behalf are a few examples of the ways an individual might invest time in the care of aging parents.

For many persons in midlife, the care of parents is a labor of love. Some are quite resistant to giving such care. Life for them has become complicated and they are too tired or distracted to provide the necessary nurture. Instead, they pull away from their parents. Those who are willing to assume the work of aiding an aging loved one must pay a significant price. The emotional strain that such care potentially adds to the midlifer and his family is not imaginary. The task of moving a senior adult into a midlife household can be complicated, especially if adolescent family members are involved.

Throughout the process of caring for parents a temptation toward stagnation can be taking place within the midlife adult. The investment of care in this new, and perhaps unexpected, responsibility may force the midlifer to experience a hopeless feeling of "I'll never get out from under this responsibility." If the person is still maneuvering for success and recognition, the addition of more family will weigh heavily.

## Adolescence

Another changing relationship that occurs in the middle years involves children who move beyond adolescence and leave home.

The problems related to this issue are legion. It is always challenging to live with adolescents. The dynamic changes through which they move are difficult to catalog. The adolescent years are a time for identity searching and questing for a direction in life. Interestingly enough, the developmental issue of adolescence is a reasonable facsimile of the issue that the midlife individual is working to resolve. The crises through which the adolescent moves often aggravate the searching process of the midlife parents with whom they are living. Parents may become resentful of their risky, questing teenager. The youthful strength and general attitude of challenging authority may prove to be a frustrating burden for parents who are experiencing their own transition.

In time, the teenager will move away from home and a totally new struggle will begin for the parent. As much discomfort as adolescent development may cause, most often it is not to be compared with the shock of the "empty nest." Teenagers may leave home under the best of circumstances, or the worst. Parents will either be thrilled or dejected over the manner in which the child leaves and the lifestyle that their offspring chooses to adopt. Whatever their feelings, the unavoidable process of reordering life without the adolescent remains. Even though an empty nest signals increased freedom for the midlife adult, with each departing child comes the growing awareness of silence and emptiness. One empty nester described the leaving of the last "chick" as an event which turned their home into "an empty cavern."

After years of nurturing children toward the goals of self-discipline and independence, parents must come to the awareness that, for better or worse, those tasks have been completed. They now move into a new relationship with their children. Hopefully, the time will come when they will stand alongside their children as friendly equals in the world of responsible adulthood. For some parents, the joy of seeing their children arrive at such a state of full responsibility will be postponed as their children live out a prolonged adolescence. Parents then must aid their young adult children in the seemingly endless process of overcoming one crisis after another. Their empty-nest pain is frustrated by the guilt of feeling "we are failures." Failure to come to terms with this changing relationship with one's children can cause a depleted spirit.

## Marital Adjustments

One of the jolting realities often faced in midlife is the awareness that the marital relationship is now in disarray. The stress of making a living, coping with parents and children, and working through one's own emotional transitions can bring damage to the fiber of a midlife marriage and leave it weakened. Hence, another changing relationship is one's marriage. Not every midlife marriage will experience a severe decline in relational effectiveness. Many maturing marriages are sturdy. Statistical data gathered from studies of marriages in the middle years, however, reflect the decay that has eroded many unattended relationships. Howard Clinebell wrote concerning the problems facing midyear couples:

> The "living happily ever after" myth is revealed as a patent fallacy in many mid-year marriages. Approximately one-fourth of the over one million couples who divorce each year in the United States have been married fifteen years or more. In the last five years, divorce among couples married twenty years or more has increased fifty percent. Most studies of marriages show a gradual disenchantment and a declining degree of marital satisfactions, especially for women, through the child-rearing years. The emotional distancing which occurs during these years often becomes permanent unless outside help is sought.[9]

Marriages cannot survive apart from the healthy environment that is created through the miracle of dialogue, flexibility, commitment, and the investment of time. Many midlifers suddenly awaken as marital strangers. Such is one of the frightening realities of middle age. The sage advice of an elderly Baptist layman seems appropriate for every marriage: "Don't forget to make a life while you are making a living." And yet, so many do forget!

Coping with the changes that come and the inevitable stresses in marriage is a primary task of midlife. Inability to do so will thrust the midlifer into a posture of stagnation and introversion. Not uncommon in the midyears are stories of extramarital affairs, over-involvement in a social life, the beginnings of alcohol or drug dependency, and workaholism. All of these may be indicators of the stagnation that has infected midlife individuals and their marriage.

Of course, not every middle-age person is married. Some have chosen to remain single. Others are single as a result of life circumstances. Singleness, however, does not relieve them of the need for intimate, supportive relationships of life. Just as the married midlifer must invest considerable energy in making marriage productive, the single adult must also nurture healthy relationships. What a tragedy to arrive at the middle of life as a loner! Stagnant, single middle-aged adults will need to move toward developing friendships. They, too, will face the battle of losing relationships of intimacy.

*Vocational Alterations*

The relationship that one has to a vocation is also in transition during the midlife growth period. Like the other crises that have entered the individual's experience, this changing relationship brings on anxiety. Few individuals move through midlife without fantasizing, planning, trying, or actualizing a change in life's work. Tired of the same routine, many persons determine at midlife to try a different approach to work that will afford them a sense of freshness and challenge. The dream that was subdued years ago now may find a way to become reality. The pressures of one's current work bring on some of this struggle, as well. Confusion in other areas of life also can feed the desire to make changes in vocational expression. Unable to breed a vital spirit into family, friendships, or one's personal life, work may be altered as a way of discovering exhilarating life.

Midlife persons often make radical changes in profession and vocation. Bureaucracy and schedules may give way to cows, dirt, and open spaces. The risk of "going it alone" seems worth it for those who are tired of being responsible to someone else. The reevaluation of one's gifts and abilities at midlife may send some back to school to prepare belatedly for the task they "should have been doing all along." Gale Sheehy calls those who move out on new vocational ventures at midlife "pathfinders."[10] There is something intriguing about those who make a successful transition. However, not all midlife work transitions are pleasant.

Some alterations in vocation are forced and not chosen. Divorce and the death of a spouse can cause a shift in one's work. Employers who find certain midlife personnel to be expendable may replace them with younger, more aggressive individuals. The rise and fall of local and national economies can force vocational transitions. Individual health and financial problems also spawn work changes. Circumstances such as these may prove to be a debilitating discouragement. Even pathfinders find their faces dirtied from the many falls that they take upon an uneven pathway. It is not easy to change one's work, voluntarily or otherwise. Grief and anxiety may be prominent emotions for those who go through the changing relationship of work. Depression may become an accepted daily countenance. Hopefully, the joy of renewal in life's calling becomes a reality.

## Changing Friendships

One final relationship change needs to be noted. In the midyears, the changing of one's intimate friendship structure is inevitable. Many of the friendships that have been present through the celebrations and valleys begin to be altered. Trusted support persons move; others divorce; still others radically alter their life philosophy and drift away ideologically. Death begins to claim some. As a result loneliness and distance can mark the lives of many middle-age adults.

Who needs friends anyway? The answer, of course, is all of us. They are a vital part of the human support and growth system. Midlifers must be in a consistent state of developing friendships, both new and old. We need the nurture that comes in having those persons outside the family who accept us as we are and encourage us in the business of becoming all we can be. The risk of moving close to others must become a learned process for the midlife adult. Even if they have lived fairly secluded lives up until this point, they need the security of other comrades in the shifting sand of their current transition.

This is not an easy task to perform, especially if one is married. The situation is made even more difficult if children are still in the homes of median adults. Friendships are nurtured in the soil of common interests, similarity in lifestyles, and the investment of time. The caring pastor and congregation will seek to be a friend. Also, they will help the community of faith to fulfill one of its most important functions, that of building relationships within the family of God. "Two are better than one, because they have a good reward for their toil. For if they fall, one will lift up his fellow; but woe to him who is alone when he falls and has not another to lift him up" (Ecclesiastes 4:9-10, RSV).

### A Summation: Tempted and Tried

Changes, changes, changes! That is, in part, what midlife is all about. On every hand, the middle-age adult is confronted with the reality of change. Each change is a temptation to stumble into a state of nongenerative living. Physical changes, changes in the goals and objectives of one's life, alterations in relationships, and a restructuring of life's power system all are threats to generativity and faith. Living by faith will not come easy for the one who dares to be authentic and generate life's important values to the following generation. The grief, anger, depression, frustration, fear, and guilt that can mark the person who journeys through the struggle of developing and living out a mature philosophy of life must be dealt with appropriately. Hope, love, faith, health, self-discipline, flexibility, forgiveness, and enthusiasm must fill the heart of the middle-age person. Finding these treasures of grace is the key to turning the midpoint of life into some of life's most creative years. Pastoral care for the people who walk in this journey of becoming must focus on pointing the way to these indispensable keystones of life.

## MINISTERING IN THE MIDDLE

How then shall we care for persons on the go throughout the afternoon of their pilgrimage? They are some of the most difficult people to reach with the message and ministry of the Gospel. Those individuals and families who have already found great security in the church will tend to be the most responsive ones to the love of church and pastor. Of course, even people of faith will resist ministry as they struggle with emotions such as shame, guilt, failure, and doubt that can be generated in their life encounters. Others who are not active participants in some faith tradition will at times be suspicious of the caring initiative that invades their sometimes struggling lives. The church and Christianity may be viewed as burdensome responsibilities that will place even greater demands on their time. The pastor could be perceived as a hovering parental/authority figure that only wants to limit their quest for happiness and fulfillment.

The distance midlife adults place at times between themselves and others can be an intimidating factor in initiating pastoral care. Folks in the middle can appear to be powerful, self-assured, angry, disinterested, busy, and withdrawn all in an effort to resist help. The bombardment of change that they are enduring may cause them to fear any further risk. The very thing they need, a growing faith, may be the reality they most resist. The known quantity of their struggle may seem better than the unknown quantity of the Gospel and Christian ministry.

### As You Begin

Several theological issues concerning ministry to the middle-age person need to be faced while formulating an approach to caring for this age group. The caring/healing processes of life are not free to do their most powerful work if the theology that undergirds ministry is inaccurate. The following issues are pivotal for midlife ministry.

### Life Can Be a Struggle

A well-known pastor/preacher once summed up life as a process that holds the potential of getting better and better while it gets harder and harder. It's true. Life can be a struggle, and quite often is. Those who would care for midlife adults must absolve themselves of all notions that the life of faith ought to be one victorious experience after another. The temptations of Jesus (see Matthew 4: 1-11) are certainly illustrative of the struggling journey called life. Temptations confront us along the way with the misconception that we can live above the suffering of life.

There is struggle involved in being a middle-age adult. Don't promise an easy pathway for them if they simply adhere to certain theological truths and principled actions in life. Truth and life's highest principles lead to the fullness of life, but they don't bypass all struggle. Each one will cope quite differently through the process of maturing. Your ministry will be stronger if you don't work out of the illusion that you can deliver middle-aged adults from the struggle. At best, you can help midlife persons to make decisions to live by faith, point them in the direction of God, and encourage them when they stumble.

As you face your own life struggles, grow in grace, and accept the reality of life's struggles, you will then learn to view pain and struggle as opportunities for growth. Paul, the apostle of Jesus, seems to teach that very truth with these words: "We rejoice in our sufferings, knowing that suffering produces endurance, and endurance produces character, and character produces hope, and hope does not disappoint us, because God's love has been poured into our hearts through the Holy Spirit which has been given to us" (Romans 5:3-5, RSV). Victory and joy are the by-products of faith. As one journeys toward the fulfillment of life, one finds that the fullness of heaven is at hand, even in our sufferings!

### *Failure Isn't Always the Product of Error and Sin*

How easy it is to label every failure as being rooted in some past sin or misguided action. No doubt, the midlife adults with whom you work will feel a deep sense of past failures for their present dilemmas. Some of their struggles are directly rooted in poor management of life and bad decision making. All of us are the products of our past in so many ways. However, there is fallacy in assuming that all present struggle is the result of a miserable past. Job in the Old Testament is a good example of a man who reaped out of proportion to his sinful ways. His "ministers'" efforts to tie his current poor standings to the past were ill-advised.

Take care not to make this common assumption. The generativity necessary for productive living among midlifers will be found, in part, as you help them to understand that all of their problems cannot be traced to the past. Help your parishioners to accept and confess their real guilt, turning to live in true repentance. Then, guide them in seeing that some of their guilt is not appropriate and real.

## Sin Can Be Forgiven

Remember, regardless of how dark the night may become for those who are searching for generativity and mature faith, there is always grace and hope. The mess which we humans make of life seems to be most messy in midlife. This is true, in part, because those in the middle years have become involved in so much of life. They have accumulated relationships, power, and commitments. Their failures seem to affect and damage so many persons. As a result, the church often does not know how to respond. The pain involved in ministering to so much trauma can be intimidating and produce within us a resistance to minister. Perhaps we are afraid that their distress will in some fashion contaminate us. In actuality, rather than being contaminated, we will discover that our efforts to reach middle-age adults in their need will reap positive results.

Following a difficult extramarital sexual affair, a man in his forties considered the prospect of dropping out of the church. Word about his involvement had spread through the community. People were shocked, hurt, and disappointed. He resigned from his positions in his church. A two-week separation occurred between the man and his spouse of nearly thirty years. Through determination, encouragement from friends, and counseling, they were able to reunite and get to work on rebuilding their lives. They began to come to church again. Before long, new rays of generativity began to blossom. After a long period of reentry to the family of faith, the man started to find ways of serving again in the church. In response to the question "How did you make it?" he replied, "God's grace and the church people just wouldn't leave me alone." Forgiveness is always a possibility! Sin can be forgiven. Indeed, it has already been forgiven in the person of Jesus Christ! Can the church do any less? Midlife ministry involves a theology of forgiveness. "Lord, how often must we forgive?" "Seven times seventy!" (see Matthew 18:21-22).

Such is not to say that we take lightly the process of sin. The God of life condemns the brokenness that destroys life. Pastors and churches will need to appropriately confront and challenge the confusion that threatens to mutilate the work of the Kingdom. Exerting pastoral initiative toward the ones who are guilty is never easy, but it must be accomplished. However, even in the midst of discipline the sounds of amazing grace should be heard.

## You Have a Ministry to Perform

How easy it is to lose sight of one's calling and authority with certain groups of folks and in some life situations. Unsure of themselves in seemingly threatening arenas of opportunity, ministers may find themselves in retreat. One of the arenas in which this often happens is midlife adulthood. We are pushed away by their struggle. We begin to question our "right" to stand with them in their need. Nagging fears about our ability to deal with the enormous complexities of ministry may become full-blown panic in the presence of midlife problems.

Coming to terms with one's calling and the source of one's personal power is a never-ending issue for ministry. Ministers must understand their own developmental struggles, stay in touch with a community of support that nurtures their sense of being, and live in the power of God's sustaining presence.[11] Remember, "God did not give us a spirit of timidity but a spirit of power and love and self-control" (2 Timothy 1:7, RSV). You have a right to express your ministry, you have been empowered for the ministry, and median adults need you.

## Nurture an Atmosphere of Hope

The beginning place for ministering to the needs of midlifers is through the development of an atmosphere of hope in your congregation. As a minister of the gospel, you operate against the backdrop of some local congregation. Most often, the middle-aged people who need your particular ministry are members of your congregation. One of the great strengths that you have to offer them (as well as those outside the congregation) is the support and environment of a covenant community. You minister as a representative of a local congregation.[12] If your work with midlifers is to be as effective as possible, you must nurture your congregation into a community that radiates the spirit of hope. In that context, your personal ministry will be hope-filled.

How does a congregation communicate hope? It does so by living in a spirit of generativity. A generative church cares about what happens in the world and is looking for ways to share the good news of God's salvation. Congregations will radiate a positive spirit of hope as they generate the truth. Those bodies of believers who have lost a sense of mission will not project an atmosphere of hope and encouragement. Hence, they will probably not have a helpful ministry to midlife adults. Middle-age adults who are discouraged and nonproductive will be encouraged to generate by being around others who are living with a spirit of generating hope.

The pastor plays a key role in the generation of hope in a church. You will want to lead your congregation to live out the truth in a risky fashion. Help them to understand the penetrating call of the gospel to go into the world with the love of Christ. Challenge them to invest in community missions that are needed. Lead them into mission causes that are far greater than your congregation, those that are worldwide in scope. To accomplish this, congregations must begin to reevaluate styles of church life that seek to turn the church into a closed society. The church of Jesus Christ has always been most valuable when it lost itself in the world.

Congregations wishing to be generative must continually ask themselves if they are only serving people like themselves, or if they are truly risking themselves with the world at large. The ever-present temptation in many congregations is to become self-serving rather than servants to a hungry, lonely world. We must remember the words of Christ, "Inasmuch as you have done it unto one of the least of these my brethren, you have done it unto me" (Matthew 25:40, NKJ). The added benefit that comes in leading a congregation to be mission minded is the encouragement such loving ministry engenders within midlife adults.

### Teach a Christian Philosophy of Generativity

Another facet of ministry to middle-age persons is to be found in teaching them the truth about midlife. Folks in the middle years need some information about this time of life. They need to know how to navigate through these uncharted waters. By now, most Americans have come to know the term *midlife crisis,* but few know the full importance of the event. Most adults have heard the myths about the adventures of midlife, but do many of them know for sure what it is really like or all about?

The pastor can help through his or her teaching ministry. The pastor is not the only one who teaches in the congregation, but this central role as pastor/teacher puts him or her in a unique position to influence the entire teaching program of the church. For one thing, the pastor's sermons should reflect a spirit that is sensitive to middle-adult life. The realities of their experience should be addressed specifically through sermons. The possibility of preaching a series on the life cycle holds great merit.[13] Also, the various teachings of most sermons could be applied specifically to the challenges of midlife, as well as to other phases of life.

In addition to sermons, the pastor can lead in developing church classes that identify the midlife task and develop the life skills needed for living as adults. No doubt, many pastors will lack the specific training and study in midlife issues to teach such a course with confidence. Enlisting the teaching services of a gifted midlife theorist might encourage the participation of your middle-age adults. Potential topics for discussion with the adults would be: developing a philosophy for living as a mature adult; living with aging parents; growing with your teenager; facing death at midlife; making the most of your vocation; family life for middle-age adults; and the middle-age adult in the church. An excellent book study for adults might be Reuel Howe's stimulating volume, *The Creative Years,* or William Hulme's *Mid-Life Crisis.*[14]

Another teaching opportunity for the pastor is found in structuring retreat settings for persons in midlife. At least once a year, congregations need to provide an outing for these individuals. Middle-age adults are one of the groups in churches that seldom go on a retreat. Retreats for adults give them the chance to pull away from the pressure of life, think about their philosophy of life, discover the encouragement of others who are going through the same struggles, and develop a refreshing spirit of Christian renewal. It could be a time for informal and formal play. They could use the retreat as an opportunity to discover again the freedom to enjoy life and run the risk of failure. Like the church classes, retreats should focus upon a wide range of topics for discussion. Marriage enrichment is a theme that needs to be addressed often in the informal atmosphere of a retreat.

The pastoral teaching role consists not only in the pastor's personal teaching, but it also finds expression through equipping others for teaching median adults. Along with preparing for their teaching experience through biblical research, Sunday school teachers should be prepared through understanding the people with whom they work. Week by week, those who teach in the middle-age adult group have the opportunity to discuss pertinent issues of life with their students. All through their Bible teaching they can dispense the truth about the ways in which the Gospel meets the particular needs of people. As you teach teachers about midlife, they will discover ways of making their teaching more relevant.

The teaching role of the pastor can be especially rewarding with midlife adults. Those adults who will submit themselves to the discipline of learning during their adult years are some of life's best learners. Adults bring a great deal of motivation, insight and accumulated knowledge, wisdom, self-discipline, and learning skills to their classroom experiences. Too many teaching pastors play down the possibility of adults being able to learn. Much effort is directed toward the children and youth of a congregation, while adults are overlooked. A good argument can be made for concentrating large amounts of pastoral energy in the direction of teaching adults. As adults mature and grow in their knowledge of life, they are able to influence the younger generation in a positive fashion.

Remember, as you teach, you are not the only one who is seeking to teach a generative philosophy to midlifers. In fact, the whole world is attempting to influence the outcome of the lives of midlifers. Multitudes of lifestyle options are presented daily to adults. The philosophies offered as a way of life have to do with wealth, power, success, and pleasure. You will want to shape a generative lifestyle that is rooted in the good soil of loving relationship with God and man. Help adults to know how to relate the gospel of grace to loving their errant children, their struggling marriage, their social involvement in life, their responsibility as citizens to the fabric of life, and the care and nurture of their own being.

### *Encourage Faith in the Midst of Crisis*

The struggles of midlife adults become clearly defined in the concrete crisis experiences through which they travel. Most do not have a clear sense of the developmental crisis that they are experiencing, but they have a vivid awareness of the day-to-day struggles that are theirs. Unless middle-age persons have chosen the road of stoicism, one can hear them voice concerns about their children's developmental problems, their own marital predicaments and joys, work and its related agenda, and the physical manifestations of their midlife. These are some of the particular crises that are the concrete expressions of middle age. The pastor must look for the midlife crisis events and seek to minister to his people in their crises.

Basically, a crisis is an occasion of distress in the life of an individual. Since persons will perceive potential stress-producing circumstances in different ways, the making of a crisis depends upon the perception of the persons who are involved in it. Pastors often are confused by events. Events appearing to be a crisis to the minister may only be a trivial matter to the parishioner. Likewise, the pastor's sense that an event is only a minor concern for the individual may be greatly in error. Spending time with people, listening to their evaluation of events, and noting the physical/emotional responses they demonstrate will aid the minister in interpreting the crisis nature of events.

## Move Toward the Person in Crisis

The pastor who hopes to share in the life of middle-age adults must meet them in the midst of their crisis experiences. It is in the midst of their crisis times that midlifers are asking the kinds of questions that can lead ultimately to a deeper faith. Armed with the truth that is being hammered out in his or her own life, the pastor can feel some confidence in becoming involved in the crisis times for adult church members. In his classic volume *The Christian Pastor*, Wayne Oates describes the pastor's ministry as one that is expressed centrally in times of crisis.[15] To be sure, there are other times in which the pastor ministers, but crises are prime times for growth in the life of an individual. The minister who seeks to share the whole of life with his or her people becomes involved in the crisis time as a respected and trusted person. As an environment of trust prevails, crisis ministry is powerful in its ability to assist persons in their growth.

Certain events seem to be predictable crises and should be so noted by those who minister. Death, sickness, hospitalization, divorce, family strife, losing or changing jobs, the departure of a child from the home, moving to a new community, and the traumatic events occurring in the lives of one's children and aging parents, are some of the more obvious dilemmas. All of these are certain to raise some level of anxiety as persons experience them. Ministers can prepare for ministry in these times of crisis by studying the characteristic human responses to such events. Preparation for caring can also be made through studying the theory and practice of ministry in each of these major crisis periods.[16]

### *Establish a Sense of Community and Concern*

The minister must encounter the person in crisis and he or she must also seek to establish some sense of caring with the individual if the individual is to grow through the traumatic experience. The establishment of concern with persons is not solely dependent upon the length of time a pastor has known someone, although a prior relationship of care is helpful. Crisis seems to demand the need for a reestablishment of care. People who hurt often withdraw from any help. Hence, the task of building relationship is made more difficult. The doorway to establishing care is through patient, reflective listening. As the parishioner senses the depth of another's concern, receptivity for ministry is increased. Persons simply must be allowed to tell their stories, and you must listen. Listening is not the finale of the healing process, simply the overture. Through this avenue you will be encouraging individuals to work toward the resolution of their problems. They will sense they are not alone in their hurt. As confidence begins to rise, you will be able to challenge them to new awareness and new levels of living. It is probably best not to give too much advice in the early stages of crisis ministry. Trying to solve their problems for them might dampen their desire to become involved in discovering the way to live and in doing it.

### *The Challenge to Decide*

Once the level of trust has been established and a person's story has been expressed, the person will need to make decisions about the present and the future. In this part of the caring process, you will be able to challenge the parishioner to make the decisions that are essential to well-being. Often, you will serve as one who confronts and challenges the person to make choices. Whether or not you use an overt manner of confrontation depends on the crisis at hand. At times, your confrontation and challenge is accomplished through the integrity of your own life and the strength of your character. Often, all you will need to do is ask, "What are you going to do about all of this?"

*Ongoing Support*

As the person begins to develop some direction in life as a result of crisis, the minister might be tempted to believe that the crisis ministry has come to conclusion. Actually, only the initial phase has transpired. As the person works on the crisis, you will need to be available to consult and encourage. Every crisis is resolved through a process. Growth comes as human beings work all the way through their hurt and dilemma. In living out the results of one's decisions, new problems arise and the crisis may intensify. The pastor must aid the parishioner in interpreting the events that are transpiring, and in finding the encouragement of God. Phone calls, brief handwritten notes, an encouraging pat on the back, and occasional visits are powerful vehicles of continuing support. The visits can be informal counseling sessions in the minister's office or brief meetings over lunch or coffee, when appropriate. Out of this environment of con-sistent concern, the person finds strength for resolving the crisis and developing a mature philosophy of life.

Middle-age adults need the ministry of encouragement in their crises. The development of their mature philosophy of life is some-thing that cannot be accomplished simply through listening to the pastor's sermons, attending retreats, and working in the church. All of these are valuable, but are incomplete by themselves. The pastor must go where the midlife person is hurting—he or she must meet the individual in the midst of the particular crises of midlife. During times of crisis, midlife adults are most vulnerable to learn and mature. All of the theory they have received from their church is finally digested or rejected in the crises of their lives. When they are ill, it is an appropriate time to talk about the process of living, struggling, and dying. Unless someone meets them at the point of their grief and guilt, they will often give in to the temptation to stagnate. When they are in the midst of family conflict, they need the pastor to practice his or her best crisis ministry. Whatever you do, practice a ministry of encouragement with midlife adults.

### Counseling Goals for Midlife Concerns

The pastor who refuses to counsel middle-age adults who seek help misses a golden opportunity to fortify the faith of searching people. As with all counselees who turn to the pastor for help, midlife persons must enter counseling with a desire to grow or the counseling process will be hampered. Those who come with such an attitude are some of the most responsive counselees a pastor will ever have the opportunity to help. Why? The middle-age person has experienced more of life, knows more of life's disappointments and pain, hopefully understands the necessity of change and adaptation, and senses the importance of time. Midlife is one of the best times in life for counseling effectiveness.

The counseling approach will, of course, vary according to the needs of each counseling situation. Listening, asking appropriate questions, weighing the alternatives available to a person in a certain situation, reflecting feelings, offering advice and guidance, confrontation, and using scripture and prayer, are all appropriate when used at the correct time in the counseling conversations. When counseling midlife adults, it is necessary to use techniques that give the greatest amount of freedom to the counselee. A heavy-handed authoritarian approach in the counseling room will possibly only delay a person's struggle. Don't be afraid to offer your opinion to the midlife searcher, but don't attempt to make your interpretation the dogma of the counselee's life.

Anger, anxiety, grief, and guilt are four major themes that will continually surface in counseling the midlife adult. The presence of these issues varies among persons, but if the counselor listens carefully these four themes will be heard. These are not unique concerns of midlife; they are experienced all through life. Even so, these issues find a uniquely powerful expression in the lives of many midlife adults. Successful counseling will address these painful agendas.

*Anger*

Anger must be faced. Counselees will appear on the pastor's doorstep seeking relief from this bitter pill. Many of them have been taught that anger must be suppressed. From childhood they have carried the belief that anger is unacceptable to God and the parent figures of their world. Others have been given the freedom to express their anger but not the wisdom to understand its origins. With rage, they lash out at their world. Regardless of how persons deal with anger, the result is the same if they do not come to terms with the source of it and learn to express it appropriately. Unresolved anger kills intimacy in relationships. It causes a person to retreat from life or to live a life of destructiveness.

The counseling room can become a helpful place for learning to express and deal with anger. The pastoral counselor helps give birth to the expression of such feelings. Once expressed, an individual is then free to investigate the origins of such strong feelings. It will do little good to tell a counselee not to be angry. The better course is to investigate the anger. The danger in counseling angry midlife church members is that they may project their anger onto the pastor if he or she is unable to help them resolve their problem, or does not agree with their philosophy of life. The pastor will need to find strength for this ministry by dealing with his or her own anger in a prayerful fashion. Such personal strength will equip the minister to face another's anger and not run from it. It will allow a caring person to firmly guide the midlife angry person toward freedom.

Anger will be one of the presenting issues in midlife marital conflict counseling. Ministers who are not equipped practically or emotionally to deal with heavy conflict among their parishioners should make healthy referrals early in the counseling contact. Midlife families seeking the pastor's counseling assistance usually have been in conflict for a long time. The level of disintegration in the family may have already progressed to the point of separation and divorce. If so, pastors will need to find the best help for their church families as soon as possible.[17] Pastors who are trained extensively in counseling and have the time to invest will work through the issues with their families who come in anger and conflict.

## Anxiety

Anxiety is another common theme of midlife counseling. Midlife adults feel pushed to the limits of existence and turn to the resource of a caring pastor. The symptoms of their anxiety may be legion and generally are rooted in a life history marked with a general sense of poor self-worth. Life threatens the anxious on every hand. As persons attempt to fight the good fight of making sense out of life, they feel overwhelmed.

Helping persons with anxiety begins with accepting them as persons of value and worth. They must feel they are acceptable to God, themselves, the pastor, and all of life. The pastoral counselor will need to let them talk through their anxiety, help them discover the sources of it, assure them of God's love and acceptance, and aid them in structuring a lifestyle that helps to defuse their anxiety. Quite generally, the middle-aged adult can be helped with anxiety problems by talking through the meaning of life and the fleeting nature of earthly existence. The fear of growing old and dying may be at the root of the anxiety. As the person learns to develop a life of prayer, worship, recreation, and intimate fellowship, his or her anxiety should become less of a threatening event.

## Grief

Grief appears in abundance at midlife. Much of it is anticipatory in nature. They are facing the loss of so much. Catch them in an open, unguarded moment, and they may open the door to the deepest thoughts of their lives and tell their fears of dying. Listen carefully and it becomes clear they are already grieving the loss of life. A large amount of their grief is reactionary. Friends and family members have begun to die by this time. Jobs have been lost, moves have been made, divorces have happened, children have left the home and turned it into an empty nest, and grief is real.

Grief has been called the wound that heals itself. Indeed, the process of grief is well documented.[18] Midlife adults, like all other human beings, have an excellent opportunity to revitalize and reinvest their energies into life as they resolve their grief. One of the major problems is the compounding of grief that comes with middle age. Too much grief can be devastating. As a result, persons can move into a state of chronic grief and atrophy. For these wounded persons, life becomes an unending experience to be endured. The hope of joy seems lost in a sea of tears and pain. It should be noted, also, that many of those who need to experience the comfort of God are persons who are walking in steps of grief that can be traced to childhood. Pastors who counsel persons in grief will seek to help them see the multiplication of grief that is taking place at the midpoint of their lives. Allowing them to verbalize the many attendant feelings such as anger, fear, and depression will allow healing to progress. The pastoral counselor seeks to aid the expression of the pain, not to suppress the pain. Grief counseling is a process which pastors must know thoroughly.[19]

## Guilt

Guilt quite often runs deep at the midpoint of life. The power to generate a productive life is being defused in many middle-age adults by the stinging reality of guilt. As the pastor traces the guilt to its source, he discovers that it is both appropriate and inappropriate guilt. It is important to distinguish between the two sources and aid the sufferer in discovering the degree of appropriateness to his or her guilt. Some are carrying an abundance of condemnation born of a heritage that communicated the person's unworthiness. Others are fighting to suppress the feelings of guilt that stem from occasions when they transgressed the right way of life.

As the pastor listens to the tales of midlife, he or she will aid persons to come to terms with their guilt. Through confession, prayer, receiving forgiveness, and determining to live a life of repentance and (in some instances) restitution, the midlife individual can begin to sing the song of salvation's joy. Take care not to assign all guilt to some real source of sin. Help the person to diagnose the source of guilt and receive the grace of God in Jesus Christ. Once the guilt is relieved, there is freedom to invest more energy into faith and generativity.

## SPIRITUAL DEVELOPMENT ISSUES

One of the unique opportunities Christian ministers and communities enjoy is the challenge of equipping God's people to increase in faith, hope, and love. Caring for the spiritual development of persons from birth to death is a complex task, indeed. Caring for the spiritual development of the midlife sojourner is perhaps the most complex opportunity of all. Their faith can be simple or complicated. They may be hardened in their resistance to the message of grace or warmly responsive to the way of Christian obedience. Some have spent a lifetime experiencing the culture and tradition of churches, others have only little exposure to faith traditions. At midlife they may have settled into routines that will make radical obedience to God difficult to embrace. On the other hand, those who find their way into ongoing spiritual growth display an enthusiasm for the way of God that can be infectious.

The central reality that must be remembered in seeking to equip midlife adults in their spiritual growth is their innate hunger for meaning and truth. They are the generation that is encountering wholeheartedly the reality of their finitude and the importance of having a philosophy of life that satisfies. In other words, they are naturally sensitive to issues that relate to the inner life. The challenge to minister among this complex age group is difficult, but the opportunity for spiritual inroads with midlife adults is magnified by their internal quest for meaning.

In seeking to understand the task of spiritual development in midlife adults, the work of James W. Fowler is crucial.[20] His stages of faith help us to see the potential for faith development in persons across a lifetime. Of the midlife adult years, he writes:

> At midlife or beyond we frequently see the emergence of the stage we call Conjunctive faith. This stage involves the embrace and integration of opposites or polarities in one's life. . . . It means realizing in one's late thirties, forties, or beyond that one is both young and old, . . . masculine and feminine, . . . (and that we are) constructive people and, inadvertently, destructive people. . .

> There are religious dimensions to the reintegration of polarities in our lives in Conjunctive faith. Here symbol and story, metaphor and myth, both from our traditions and from others, seem to be newly appreciated, in what Paul Ricoeur has called

a second or willed naivete. Having looked critically at traditions and translated their meanings into conceptual under-
standings, one experiences a deeper relationship to the reality
that symbols mediate.[21]

Of course, not every median adult finds himself or herself at such
a profound level of faith. Having failed to move beyond some of the
earlier levels of faith development, adults often struggle across a
lifetime with a faith that doesn't fit their need. They have not
learned to pray "I do believe, help me overcome my unbelief!"
(Mark 9:24b, NIV). Even so, the natural hunger for meaning ex-
pands during midlife and the church must respond in helping them
to find more of God.

### *Introductions to the Way, the Truth, and the Life*

As middle-age adults become immersed in their quest for a
meaningful life, the church has a profound opportunity to introduce
the message of Christ. One of the truths we should never forget is
the reality that people, regardless of age, need the transforming love
of God that is found in a real and personal relationship with Christ.
Somewhere in the midst of the upsetting crises that come to midlifers, surely there is an avenue for thinking and considering the
person of Jesus Christ and the way of life he offers. Hopefully,
congregations are ready for such conversations as members and
ministers, of all ages, internalize the truth of the Gospel and learn to
relate their lives to others.

The best evangelism is always relational. Losses that bombard
midlifers can be overcome, in part, through the love and genuine
friendship of God's people. Each person in God's family has a
network of relations in the community where they reside, work,
shop, and play. As people of faith build friendships with middle-age
adults, they are paving the pathway for faith awakenings that lead to
genuine life conversion.[22]

The intellectual and philosophical development of persons in
midlife should dictate greatly the approach followed for helping
persons toward faith in God. One kind (or strategy) of evangelism
doesn't fit all adults. The best evangelism relates the Gospel to the

life maturity and life circumstances of individuals. Some will find their way into the Kingdom through intellectual avenues that are similar to those followed by C. S. Lewis, while others will discover faith through the blinding light and simple surrender of a man such as Saul of Tarsus.[23]

## Finding Faith in Fellowship

Perhaps the most important aspect of helping middle-age adults to develop spiritual strength is Christian fellowship. Keep remembering that Jesus called his disciples out of a world of alienation and into a communion of love and holiness.[24] The apostle Paul gave his life to the business of starting and nurturing churches into life. It does seem obvious in the New Testament that people of faith were intended to live in a community of faith. In the beginning they were drawn together to celebrate his mighty acts of history as they worshipped, grow in faith as they studied the scriptures, and care for one another as they reached out to the world in common witness of their faith.

Wayne Oates has observed, however, that "the middle years are often a time when the person narrows down his range of relationships rather than widening the range to include new people and deepening it to enrich the relationships he already has."[25] That being true, the church faces a challenge with many midlife adults in discovering ways for helping them to experience the enrichment of Christian fellowship. Stimulating and creative corporate worship encounters will help to draw midlifers into worship experiences. Most will find large group encounters more tolerable than small group experiences. Rare is the adult who will seek out intimate growth groups where they are strangers. Traditional church classes may not be the answer for Christian nurture in the strength of a small group. Perhaps the avenue of home-based growth groups is the key to reaching midlife adults. As they are drawn into fellowship in the friendly confines of homes where they meet friends and think together of faith intersecting life, they can be more open and experience the openness of their friends and loved ones.

Midlife adults need the benefits found in friendship and the community of faith. They would do well to find the reality that theologian Deitrich Bonhoeffer discovered in his prison cell during the early 1940s: the indispensable nature of "life together." The face and embrace of God become stronger for adults in communion and community.

## Learning to Love a Quiet Place

Busy adults are always in need of learning the value of a quiet place—a place for being alone and for listening to the "still small voice" of God's Spirit. Like Elijah the prophet (I Kings 18-19), midlife adults are often depleted by the battles of life. Some have lived far too long on the empty quest for meaning in business, power, wealth, and pleasure. Sooner or later, the candle that has been burning at both ends goes out and real despair can settle over depleted souls.

The value of teaching adults the way of deliberate, systematic quietness is significant. Midlifers are excellent prospects for the philosophical struggles that accompany contemplative prayer, scripture meditation, fasting, and lonely retreats. Even those persons who have studied the Bible and prayed throughout their lives would benefit from an immersion in the disciplines of the soul.[26] Special consideration should be given to preparing individuals within the church who are able to mentor midlifers in the way of quietness.

As midlife persons let themselves be surrounded by the reality of God's presence, they begin to hear truths that will challenge their status quo. In the lonely place, a light in the soul can be turned on and hope for the future, grace for the past, and strength for the day can be embraced.

## 'Tis a Gift to Be Simple

Spiritual development is more than an inward matter for everyone who seeks a deeper way of life. Midlife adults are especially needful of a pathway for simple service that leads beyond themselves. Complicated lives benefit from cutting out the unnecessary and trivial in favor of focusing simply upon lasting values. Learning to live as lilies of the field and birds of the air is truly an important lesson for the person who struggles with the meaning of life.

Those who will listen to the voice of compassion calling them beyond self-centeredness will find the face of Jesus. "Inasmuch as you've done it unto the least of these. . . . you've done it unto me," Jesus said (Matthew 25:40, NKJ). Hence, the church must be in the business of calling the faithful to find the joy of servanthood and life as Jesus lived it. Helping midlife adults to become better stewards of life's resources (time, talents, and treasure) will be a challenge (but a necessity) as they often must face up to their need for reordering long-established priorities. The church also will want to help them learn a way past generalized and diffused compassion that only feels the troubles of the world at large, so that they might discover the joys of becoming good Samaritans caring for some particular, singular need that is their calling and responsibility.

Midlife is a wonderful time to assess the spiritual gifts that God has granted each person for service. Using these talents to live is far better than simply trying to find a place to fit in. As midlifers discover the gifts and callings that God is providing, the encouragement of the church will be a necessity as they make big leaps of faith into new ventures of living. Middle-age adults would do well to move from "success to significance,"[27] investing in those avenues of life that would help them to realize the satisfaction of faithful discipleship, even if it meant changing vocations or jobs. Surely some of the most important service opportunities for this age group will be those that bring them into servant roles with persons younger than themselves. After all, this is the generation that is charged with the task of passing along life's wisdom to the generations that follow.

## CONCLUSION

Of his own midlife journey, Howard Clinebell wrote: "From a perspective halfway through the years from forty to sixty-five, I can say that the mid-years to date have been the most fulfilling and productive period of my life. They also have been a time of painful problems and accelerating losses."[28] Such is the reality of life in the middle. Painful, yes. Hopefully however, it is also the most fulfilling and productive time of life that people have lived. It can be just that if persons are able to develop a mature philosophy of life that makes sense out of all the challenges, successes, problems, pains, and losses. The church of Jesus Christ has a lot to say about the possibility of developing such a good life. Through teaching, encouraging, counseling, and nurturing faith, ministers and caring churches can help midlife adults experience personal growth and a deeper faith while they are getting it together in life!

## NOTES

1. Levinson, Daniel J., et al. *The Seasons of a Man's Life.* New York: Ballantine Books, 1970; Gail Sheehy, *Passages: Predictable Crises of Adult Life.* New York: Bantam Books, 1977. Sheehy has continued throughout the years as a prolific researcher and writer on midlife adulthood. See Sheehy's *New Passages: Mapping Your Life Across Time.* New York: Ballantine Books, 1996; *Menopause: The Silent Passages,* Revised and Updated. New York: Pocket Books, 1995; and *Understanding Men's Passages: Discovering the New Map of Men's Lives.* New York: Random House, 1998.

2. Howe, Reuel L. *The Creative Years: A Mature Faith for Adult Life.* New York: The Seabury Press, 1959.

3. Sherrill, Lewis J. *The Struggle of the Soul.* New York: Macmillan Publishing Co., Inc., 1959, p. 150.

4. Levinson, p. 60.

5. Sheehy, *Passages*, p. 364.

6. Ibid., p. 350.

7. Wiersbe, Warren W. Mid-life Crises? Bah, Humbug! *Christianity Today* (May 21, 1982), p. 26.

8. Sheehy, *Passages*, p. 356.

9. Clinebell, Howard J. Jr. *Growth Counseling for Mid-Years Couples.* Philadelphia: Fortress Press, 1977, p. 22.

10. Sheehy, *The Pathfinders.* New York: William Morrow and Co., Inc., 1981.

11. Paul, Cecil R. See *Passages of a Pastor.* Grand Rapids, MI: Zondervan Publishing House, 1981; and Louis McBurney, *Every Pastor Needs a Pastor.* Waco, TX: Word Books, 1977, for excellent help in coming to terms with the stresses and personal needs of a pastor. Likewise, C. W. Brister's *Caring for the Caregivers.* Nashville: Broadman Press, 1985, is filled with wisdom that will help ministers in understanding ways to find a stronger sense of self in fulfilling their calling from God.

12. Oates, Wayne E. *The Christian Pastor,* Third Edition, Revised. Philadelphia: The Westminster Press, 1982, pp. 89-91.

13. Claypool, John. See *Stages: The Art of Living the Expected.* Waco, TX: Word Books, 1977, for a sample series of sermons on the developmental stages of life.

14. Howe, Reuel. *The Creative Years.* New York: Seabury Press, 1959; and William E. Hulme. *Mid-Life Crisis.* Philadelphia: The Westminster Press, 1980.

15. Oates, pp. 17-64.

16. Brister, C. W. See *Pastoral Care in the Church*, Third Edition, Revised and Expanded. San Francisco: Harper, 1992, pp. 208-263; and Marcus D. Bryant. *The Art of Christian Caring*. St. Louis, MO: The Bethany Press, 1979, for helpful summaries on caring during the crisis moments of life.

17. Oglesby, William B. *Referral in Pastoral Counseling*. Philadelphia: Fortress Press, 1968; and Wayne E. Oates and Kirk H. Neely's *Where to Go for Help*, Revised and Enlarged Edition. Philadelphia: Westminster Press, 1972. Helpful clues on making positive referrals.

18. Bailey, Robert W. See *The Minister and Grief*. New York: Hawthorn Books, 1976, for a summary analysis of grief and the pastor's role in grief work.

19. Oates, Wayne E. *Pastoral Care and Counseling in Grief and Separation*. Philadelphia: Fortress Press, 1976. An invaluable volume for understanding the process of counseling with those who grieve.

20. Fowler, James W. See *Stages of Faith: The Psychology of Human Development and the Quest for Meaning*. San Francisco: Harper and Row, 1981; *Becoming Adult, Becoming Christian: Adult Development and Christian Faith*. San Francisco: Harper and Row, 1984; and *Weaving the New Creation: Stages of Faith and the Public Church*. San Francisco: HarperCollins, 1991.

21. Fowler, *Weaving*, p. 111.

22. My father became a professing Christian in his early forties. He was a man searching for meaning in his life during those years. Following World War II and several years of government service, he and my mother, along with their three children, moved to Houston, Texas. He was working at a job that didn't suit him, confused in his personal identity, and anxious about the future well-being of his family. In a time of deep personal and family crisis, a friend who cared (a barber who often cut his hair) introduced my father to the story of Jesus and the fellowship of a church family. With the simple faith of a child (probably James Fowler's "mythic-literal faith") he began a pilgrimage of faith that transformed the fabric of my family's life. I am a debtor to a simple man of faith who found my father in the crisis of midlife and introduced him to the Way, the Truth, and the Life.

23. Hinson, William H. See *A Place to Dig In: Doing Evangelism in the Local Church*. Nashville: Abingdon Press, 1987, for a helpful discussion on the key role of evangelism in church life.

24. The Greek word used in the New Testament for church, [εκκισία], means "called out ones."

25. Oates, Wayne E. *When Religion Gets Sick*. Philadelphia: The Westminster Press, 1970, p. 96.

26. The works of Richard E. Foster are superb for teaching spiritual disciplines to persons. See especially *The Challenges of the Disciplines Life*. San Francisco: HarperCollins, 1985; *Celebration of Discipline: The Path to Spiritual Growth*. San Francisco: Harper and Row, 1988. Also see Morton T. Kelsey, *The Other Side of Silence: A Guide to Christian Meditation*. New York: Paulist Press, 1976.

27. Buford, Bob. See *Halftime: Changing Your Game Plan from Success to Significance*. Grand Rapids, MI: Zondervan, 1994, for an encouraging story of a

man who found new meaning in the halftime of life as he moved beyond a very successful career to found Leadership Network, a far-reaching organization geared to helping churches prepare for successful ministry in the twenty-first century.

28. Clinebell, p. 1.

## ANNOTATED BIBLIOGRAPHY

Brister, C. W. *The Promise of Counseling.* San Francisco: Harper and Row, Publishers, 1978.

> Written by one of the strongest contributors to the study of pastoral care in our day. This book is a guide for understanding the indispensable principles of pastoral counseling. A good overview for pastors.

Coleman, Lucien E. Jr. *Understanding Adults.* Nashville: Convention Press, 1969.

> This is a simple volume that helps to bring valuable insight to the process of educating adults. Coleman writes for church educators, but brings an uncomplicated wisdom that lay persons will find helpful in learning the way of adult education.

Foster, Richard J. *Celebration of Discipline: The Path to Spiritual Growth. Revised Edition.* San Francisco: Harper and Row, 1988.

> This is Foster's magnum opus on spirituality. He helps us to learn the practical disciplines of faith. Adults will benefit from the content of this volume because it amplifies both the personal and corporate disciplines needed for growth as a Christian.

Fowler, James W. *Stages of Faith: The Psychology of Human Development and the Quest for Meaning.* San Francisco: Harper and Row, 1981.

> Every minister among adults ought to wrestle with this important volume. Fowler's work helps us to understand the characteristics of the various levels of faith. Ministry with median adults is strengthened through the understanding that Fowler brings to the ways in which people express their faith.

Gleason, John J. Jr. *Growing Up to God: Eight Steps in Religious Development.* Nashville: Abingdon Press, 1975.

> One of the best little books ever written on the developmental nature of persons and faith. Gleason uses the psychosocial construct of Eric Erickson to trace religious development.

Hinson, E. Glenn. *A Serious Call to a Contemplative Lifestyle.* Philadelphia: The Westminster Press, 1974.

> This is a very inspiring and helpful book that will assist in developing the life of devotion within midlife adults. A useful listing of practical aids to devotion is contained near the end.

Sheehy, Gail. *Understanding Men's Passages: Discovering the New Map of Men's Lives.* New York: Random House, 1998.

> Sheehy is a popularizer of developmental theory. True to her form, the book is loaded with excellent research and many illustrations and case studies. Her research gives us enormous insights into the psyche of men in our time.

Stagg, Frank. *The Bible Speaks on Aging.* Nashville: Broadman Press, 1981.

> This book is loaded with biblical teachings on the process of aging. For preaching and teaching, this is a most valuable resource.

# Chapter 6

# Senior Adulthood:
# Twilight or Dawn?

### Albert L. Meiburg

While I was in my fifties, two of my senior friends retired. I had followed their careers with keen interest, not only because they were friends, but also because I needed to plan for my own later years. I learned a lot by watching how each approached this transition from quite different perspectives.

Harold almost seemed oblivious to his approaching retirement. So far as I could tell, he was expecting to continue his business indefinitely into the future. However, it seemed to me he was ignoring some significant issues. He had a number of vague physical symptoms that eluded the doctor. He looked chronically tired. He complained about not being able to remember the names of his customers as well as he had in the past. Minor frustrations, such as getting a parking ticket, became major preoccupations.

Harold seemed stuck in a rut. On one hand, his complaints suggested he was under stress. On the other hand, he seemed to prefer to ignore his stress rather than do something about it. For example, he turned down several opportunities to make business arrangements that would have given him some income while allowing him to reduce his daily workload. His reluctance to make any changes in his life suggested to me that he was afraid of impending change.

The future can be scary at any age. Teenagers, while often excited by the prospect of adult privileges, are at the same time frightened by adult responsibilities. Some senior adults, such as Harold, equate aging with decline. Retirement can be a threat if it only means the loss of the satisfactions of working. Seniors with this outlook seem to think of aging as the close of day—*twilight*. Can you blame them for not wanting to rush toward the sunset?

Murray's approach to retirement was about as different from Harold's as day is from night. On several occasions he discussed with me various options he had under consideration. Twenty years before he reached retirement age, he bought a piece of worn-out farm land and planted fast-growing trees, as part of his financial plan for retirement.

Murray, like Harold, had some health concerns. About a year before he had planned to retire, an old illness flared up. I thought perhaps he would decide to retire sooner. Little chance! He stuck with his doctors, but kept up a reduced work schedule. Gradually his symptoms subsided.

Murray took delight in planning his retirement party. He invited many old friends. He reminisced about the struggles of his earlier years, took a lot of good-natured ribbing about his peculiarities, and shared some of his hopes for the future. A firm in a nearby city had invited him to do some consulting. He was considering running for town council.

Murray was aware of the hazards of old age, but he did not dwell on them. His response was to take the initiative. As he entered a new phase of his life, the image which seemed to guide him was that of a new day—*dawn*. He seemed to be moving forward with hope.

I wondered why the same event could evoke such contrasting attitudes. Then, it occurred to me that each of us is a unique person with his or her own genetic makeup. From each child's unique birth order in the family and continuing throughout life, an infinite variety of experiences shapes the life of the individual. Thus, the longer they live, the more diverse people tend to become. Senior adults are not stamped out with a cookie cutter!

Older people tend to cope with aging pretty much like they have dealt with life issues in preceding stages. Some, like Harold, fear the dark. Others, like Murray, believe with Zechariah that "at evening time it shall be light."[1] However, these are not the only alternatives. There is a continuum of perspectives, of which twilight and dawn symbolize the polarities.

Can we generalize about older people, given their uniqueness and individuality? While we must always be cautious in applying the general characteristics of a group to any one individual, we can identify some issues that are fairly common in later life. As we have seen, people may respond to them differently, but an understanding of the developmental tasks that face older people can alert us to their needs.

## THE DEVELOPMENTAL TASKS
## OF SENIOR ADULTHOOD

For many years the literature of human development focused almost exclusively on childhood and adolescence, with little attention to adulthood, and none to aging. The example of the pioneer American psychologist, G. Stanley Hall, who wrote significant early works on both adolescence *and* senescence, was not followed by his successors.

In the sixties and seventies, this picture began to change as both scholarly and popular writers attempted to describe adult development and the psychology of maturity.

The first studies on aging by behavioral scientists arose from concern with the unmet needs of the elderly, according to Neugarten.[2] This lead to a problem-centered view, not unlike the way in which Freud's practice with neurotics influenced the perspective of psychoanalysis. However, as research findings began to multiply and more representative samples of older people were studied, the great diversity of the patterns of successful aging became apparent.

### *The Concept of Developmental Tasks*

During the 1930s and early 1940s, educators were interested in discovering the best time for learning various skills, such as reading. They found a parallel between the concept of the "critical period" in the development of the embryo and the "readiness" of individuals to undertake certain learning tasks.

A significant model of development emerged in the concept of the "developmental task." According to Robert J. Havighurst, one of its well-known proponents, developmental tasks arise from three sources: physical maturation, cultural pressures, and the aspirations and values of the individual. In his classic definition of the "teachable moment," Havighurst incorporates all three sources: "When the body is ripe, the society requires, and the self is ready to achieve a certain task, the teachable moment has come."[3]

## Developmental Tasks of Later Life

If children grow mentally, emotionally, and socially in a predictable sequence, reasoned some behavioral scientists, why shouldn't adults do likewise? What began as the field of "child development" was broadened to "human development." Various authorities have attempted to identify the developmental tasks of later life. The following is a brief summary of some of their findings.

Havighurst was among the earliest to spell out the growth issues in middle age and later maturity. Here are the tasks he suggested as central to later life:[4]

1. Adjusting to decreasing physical strength and health.
2. Adjusting to retirement and reduced income.
3 Adjusting to the death of one's spouse.
4. Establishing an affiliation with one's age group.
5. Maintaining civic and social obligations.
6. Establishing satisfactory housing arrangements.

Evelyn M. Duvall, who studied with Havighurst at Chicago, applied the developmental task concept to families. She developed a text in family life education that showed how the family has a lifecycle of its own, and how the tasks of family members interact. Her list of the tasks of older couples includes some, but not all, of Havighurst's items. She added some tasks not given by Havighurst:[5]

1. Finding a satisfying home for the later years.
2. Adjusting to retirement income.
3. Establishing comfortable household routines.
4. Nurturing each other as husband and wife.
5. Facing bereavement and widowhood.
6. Maintaining contact with children and grandchildren.
7. Caring for elderly relatives.

8. Keeping an interest in people outside the family.
9. Finding meanings in life.

Erik H. Erikson, like Havighurst, envisioned a life-long scheme of developmental challenges. However, instead of a "list" of tasks, he sought to define *one* main issue for each life stage. If one has not "done his or her homework" for a particular stage, he or she may continue to work on it in the next stage, although this results in complications. The tasks are stated in terms of opposing tendencies.

Erikson considers the essential task of later life to be the achievement of ego-integrity versus a sense of despair.[6] By "integrity" he means a basic acceptance of one's life as having been inevitable, appropriate, and meaningful.

Failure to accomplish this task is responsible for the fear of death (despair), the feeling that time has run out, that there is no chance to start life over. On the other hand, the achievement of integrity produces the "virtue" of wisdom, which Erikson defines as "the detached and yet active concern with life itself in the face of death itself."[7]

There is an important connection, in Erikson's thought, between the eighth and final stage of growth and the key task of the preceding stage (midlife)—generativity versus stagnation. As he puts it, "Only in him who in some way has taken care of things and people and has adapted himself to the triumphs and disappointments adherent to being the originator of others or the generator of products and ideas—only in him may gradually ripen the fruit of these seven stages. I know of no better word for it than integrity."[8]

Robert C. Peck noted that Erikson's eighth stage summed up all the psychological crises of the last forty to fifty years of life. Following Erikson's pattern of opposing tendencies, he defined three tasks for old age:[9]

1. *Ego differentiation versus work-role preoccupation.* When the last child leaves home, parents have to find a replacement for parenting as a basis for selfhood. Similarly, retirement requires individuals to define themselves in ways other than their traditional work roles.

2. *Body transcendence versus body preoccupation.* In the course of normal aging, all of us will face some sort of physical

limits. Peck asks whether we will allow the physical changes associated with aging to dominate our lives, or whether we can still find challenge and satisfaction in creative mental activities and human relationships.

3. *Ego transcendence versus ego preoccupation.* Old age brings with it the certain prospect of personal death. The choice, as Peck sees it, is between passive resignation to the inevitable on one hand and a deep, active effort to make life better for those who come after, on the other.

Figure 6.1 gives a simplified overview of the perspectives of the authorities cited above. While terms may vary, there is a considerable amount of agreement. Something of a consensus emerges. Three of the four sources identify the issues of health status, retirement, and meaning in life as key tasks.

FIGURE 6.1. Developmental Tasks of Later Life According to Various Authorities

| TASKS | Havighurst | Duvall | Erikson | Peck |
|---|---|---|---|---|
| 1. Adjusting to decreasing physical health and strength | X | | | X |
| 2. Adjusting to retirement and reduced income | X | X | | X |
| 3. Adjusting to death of spouse | X | X | | |
| 4. Affiliating with one's age group | X | | | |
| 5. Meeting social and civil responsibilities | X | X | | |
| 6. Establishing satisfactory housing arrangements | X | X | | |
| 7. Finding meaning in life in the face of death | | X | X | X |
| 8. Nurturing one another as husband and wife | | X | | |
| 9. Maintaining contact with children and grandchildren | | X | | |
| 10. Caring for elderly relatives | | X | | |

## Developmental Tasks and Pastoral Care

What is the relevance of these developmental tasks for pastoral care? A developmental perspective informs and enhances pastoral care in three ways: (a) it broadens our understanding of the aging process; (b) it identifies specific growth needs of individuals; and (c) it suggests a central focus for the caring process.

One way a developmental perspective informs pastoral care is by disclosing the many faces of aging. Too often we see the last stage of life in only one dimension—the dimension of physical decline. An ancient example of this face of aging is given by the "philosopher" Ecclesiastes in these words:

> Then your arms, that have protected you will tremble, and your legs, now strong, will grow weak. Your teeth will be too few to chew your food, and your eyes too dim to see clearly. Your ears will be deaf to the noise of the street. You will barely be able to hear the mill as it grinds or music as it plays, but even the song of a bird will wake you from sleep. You will be afraid of high places, and walking will be dangerous. Your hair will turn white; you will hardly be able to drag yourself along, and all desire will be gone.[10]

The spectrum of developmental tasks makes it clear that coping with inevitable physical limitations is by no means the only challenge of later life. It may be the most obvious, but that doesn't make it the most important. Notice that of the ten tasks listed in the table, at least six (numbers 3, 4, 5, 8, 9, 10) require one to relate to other persons in some way. The social matrix of aging is obviously important.

A second way in which a developmental approach supports pastoral care is by providing a diagnostic framework. A review of the common developmental tasks can indicate the specific growing edges of a particular person at a particular time. Caring can then proceed with a clear sense of direction.

A third way in which developmental understanding enhances pastoral care is by suggesting a central focus for the caring process. For example, if we follow Erikson's scheme, we take the primary goal of our care to be encouraging the person in the pursuit of meaning (ego integrity). This means supporting persons as they come to terms with their limits, as they celebrate the joy and wisdom they have garnered, and as they discover ways to keep on living and growing.

A knowledge of the landscape of later life is to pastoral care what a road map is to a traveler. When we care for older adults we are sharing for a while their journey of faith. We may not know every turn in the road, but we know the direction and the destination. The remainder of this chapter explores the process of caring in more specific ways.

## PASTORAL CARE WITH SENIOR ADULTS

How can pastoral care be offered effectively with senior adults in the light of developmental perspectives? Effective pastoral care requires (1) an understanding of the spiritual challenges of later life, (2) an awareness of the assumptions that we bring to pastoral care, and (3) goals for pastoral care that are appropriate to the life situation of elders.

### Spirituality in Later Life

Most older Americans take their faith seriously. One survey showed that 80 percent of persons aged sixty-five or older belong to a church or synagogue, and 52 percent worship weekly. Ninety percent of seniors say they pray frequently when facing personal problems.[11]

Such studies may tell us about "religious" identity, behavior, or affiliation, but they do not necessarily shed light on "spirituality." Religion usually refers to the outward practices of faith, whereas spirit is that inward part of the self by which we come to know and experience God. Many persons who deny being "religious," would agree to being "spiritual." So spirituality is broader than the expressions of organized religion.[12]

What is the significance of research confirming the importance of spirituality for older persons?

One implication of these findings is that pastoral care is usually welcomed by most elders. However, that does not mean that all elders are spiritual giants, nor that they make the best use of the resources of faith.

The spirituality of aging is not a mystical gift that arrives along with a Medicare card on one's sixty-fifth birthday! Certainly not all senior adults have an explicitly religious view of life, nor a personal experience of God.

It may be more realistic to say that most older people have an openness toward faith, and that all can be encouraged to grow spiritually. Unfortunately, it is often assumed that older people are set in their ways and not open to change. One morning a long black car drove up in front of a church. The chauffeur asked if the pastor could speak with his ninety-year old passenger. The passenger was ushered into the pastor's study, where he asked, "Do you think the Lord has any use for an old sinner like me?" In due course, he was baptized. There is no age limit on spiritual growth!

Indeed, the experience of aging may be a harbinger of spiritual growth. Whether or not the potential for growth is realized depends upon several factors, of which one is the lifestyle and value system of the individual. As they age, some persons will face challenges strengthened by their faith. Others may have resources, but have not claimed them, while still others may have underdeveloped spiritual resources.

Even when the pastor is welcomed, unless he or she takes seriously the task of spiritual encourager, the older adult may be left only with emotional support. For some elders, realizing their growth potential at various stages of aging may depend on whether they are related to a spiritually aware and developmentally informed pastor.

Each of the focal tasks of aging noted by Peck presents the individual with options. It is in that process of making choices (and defining the self) that spirituality of later life is lived out, as we shall see later in greater detail.

### Guiding Assumptions

We bring to ministry certain assumptions about the task, about those it involves, and about ourselves. Often these assumptions are unexamined and unarticulated. You may find it helpful to try to state for yourself three or four principles you believe could serve as guidelines for your care with senior adults. I suggest the following:

## *Caregivers Must Come to Terms with Their Own Aging*

For pastoral care to be effective, the agent, pastor or lay caregiver, must be emotionally available to the person being cared for. In the context of senior adulthood, this means that caregivers must have taken a deliberate look at their feelings about their own aging. Some caregivers make overly optimistic assumptions about older people, taking such euphemisms as "golden years" too literally. While an essentially positive attitude toward aging is helpful, it should not blind us to the pain and struggles of aging.

On the other hand, some caregivers make overly pessimistic assumptions about aging, seeing only its sufferings and ignore its growth possibilities. If we define aging only as a painful prelude to death, the dread of our own aging can cause us to avoid those who remind us of our own future. For this reason, some ministers devote as little time as possible to elder ministry.

The significance of one's own feelings about aging for pastoral care was illustrated for me when "Wallace," a seminary student, showed up in my course, "Ministry with Older Persons." Wallace shared with me that he had enrolled in the course because of his dislike of older people. He traced this to his childhood when a grandparent living in his home made life miserable for him and his parents.

With my encouragement, Wallace became a volunteer chaplain in a nursing home. As he began to examine his reluctance to relate to older people his attitude began to change. He became interested in a mute resident of the home. One day, while he visited with her, she opened her eyes and spoke to him! This was a turning point. After completing seminary, he did further study in gerontology and became a minister to senior adults.

## *Caring "With" Is Better Than Caring "For"*

A preposition is a small word, but sometimes it can make a big difference in meaning. Caring "for" implies that the recipient of care is to some extent dependent. By contrast, caring "with" connotes a sense of comradeship and mutuality.

Some adults think that when they reach sixty-five, they should withdraw from "active life" and let younger people "take over." In this case, caring "for" reinforces passivity and disengagement.

The concept of caring "with" assumes that senior adults are capable of self-direction, decision making, and caring for others. When we care "with" we support autonomy and dignity.

A good indication of whether we are caring "with" or caring "for" older people is the degree to which senior adults are participants in planning and conducting the church's ministries with senior adults.[13] Seeking the wisdom of the elders of the church in program planning says to them that they are significant, and have responsibility in the life of the church.

## *Caring with Seniors Must Address the Whole Family*

Janet had looked forward to retirement for some time. After a busy career she was hoping for the freedom to travel, visit friends, and enjoy a more leisurely pace. Janet's mother had looked forward to Janet's retirement also, but for different reasons. She had lived by herself in the rambling farmhouse since her husband died years before, but now she was too feeble to continue without assistance.

In the face of her mother's needs, Janet felt she had no choice but to defer her own plans. She sold her house in the city and moved back "home." Her mother expected Janet's total attention. To her pastor, Janet confessed, "I love Mother, but I am frustrated, angry, and depressed. If I try to make the farm *my* home, Mother objects, yet she insists I must be there all the time!"

Here we have a real-life example of the importance of the assumption, that in caring for seniors, we must address the family, and not just the older person in isolation. In this situation, the needs of the "young-old" daughter are in conflict with those of her "old-old" mother. Pastoral care must take into account the needs of both.

Janet's dilemma is an increasingly common concern of younger senior adults today: how to maintain their own life and health while sustaining their aging parents. Several facts underscore the importance of family issues for informed caring:

Most older people have families who care for them and with whom they are in fairly frequent communication. The impression that most older people are neglected by their children has been shown by a number of studies to be untrue.[14]

Other older people are without children and need a substitute. Emotional support can be provided by friends, extended kin, and by the church.

The role of caregiver to aging parents is most often assigned to women. In a day when 60 percent of American women are employed outside the home, many feel severely burdened by this since they may still have adolescent children at home as well. Effective caring must be sensitive to the impact of aging on the whole family structure.

## Caring Includes Mobilizing the Available Resources

Arnold had been a widower for twelve years before developing an incurable brain disease. He had no children, but Arnold's friends at work rallied around him. At first, while his limitations were mild, they kept him included in things by driving him to work and by assigning him routine tasks he could still do.

There came a time, however, when it was necessary for him to retire because of his disability. Even then, his friends stood by him. One came by weekly to help him pay his bills. Another occasionally took him out for a meal. A third took him along when he went to the barber shop.

For almost a year, Arnold was able to remain in his own home because of the heroic efforts of his "family," along with such community support as Meals-on-Wheels and a paid companion. Arnold's needs were so diverse and so great that no single person or agency alone could have met them. Caring for Arnold required a team effort.

Caring for senior adults is usually more effective when it is approached as a team effort rather than single-handedly. If you feel overwhelmed by the needs of a senior adult, consider enlisting the aid of others: family, friends, or community agency. For assistance in discovering the resources in your community, contact your area agency on aging.

From reflection on guiding assumptions of care, we now turn to the practice of ministry.

## Goals of Pastoral Care

The goal of pastoral care is to challenge senior adults to discover the growth possibilities before them and to sustain and encourage them through the resources of their faith. Since the needs of the newly retired differ from those in their eighties and beyond, the underlying goal of pastoral care is pursued in ways appropriate to each of three senior adult stages.

### Enablement and Challenge:
### Caring with "Young" Seniors

Pastoral care with "young seniors" follows the themes of enablement and challenge. By "enablement," I mean the pastor's encouragement of continued participation in church and community. By "challenge," I mean the pastor's effort to stimulate personal growth and development.

Retirement from the workforce is a significant passage in the life cycle, yet for some it is ambiguous. Many Americans look forward to it as a reward for a lifetime of hard work. At the same time, they may dread its connotation of being "put on the shelf."

We have no rite of passage except for the "retirement dinner" and we don't even have that for women whose careers are those of mother and homemaker. John Westerhoff and William Willimon have offered thoughtful suggestions for a worship service to acknowledge retirement.[15] Such a service would seek to interpret this event in the light of the Gospel, to affirm the continuing personhood of those retiring, and to dramatize the challenges and opportunities of their new life. However, until the church has led people to approach the significant changes in their lives from the perspective of faith, simply holding recognition services is not likely to be very meaningful.

When the individual has some voice about the actual beginning of retirement, has some sort of financial security, and is in reasonably good health, the prospect is likely to be one of a welcomed sense of freedom.

Affirming this freedom, and exploring its meaning for the about-to-be and the newly retired, is an appropriate form of enablement in this phase of aging. Take Vivian, for example.

A widow with no children, Vivian had been very happy in her career with a national company. Her husband had owned his own business. After his death, she continued her own work, remained in their home, and enjoyed her church friends. However, when she became eligible for early retirement, she decided to move back to her home state to be near her brothers and sisters.

For Vivian, retirement seems to be going well. She bought a nice condominium and some new furnishings. Her health is good. She keeps in touch with her family, makes occasional trips by car to visit out-of-state friends, and does volunteer work. Vivian is typical of today's new generation of energetic "young-old" folks who are confident, useful, and happy.

Pastoral care with Vivian would include affirming her freedom and exploring her goals for retirement. The pastor in the community to which she retired could introduce her to those in the church who would include her in activities and help her discover ways in which her talents and interests could be useful to both the church and the community. She might be enlisted as a member of the senior adult council to aid in planning a balanced program of Bible study, educational, recreational, and outreach ministries as Horace Kerr has suggested.[16]

Senior adults in certain professions are able to manage their retirements as a process rather than as an event. They work out a gradual reduction in demands at a pace with which they are comfortable. This gives them both a desired sense of freedom and the satisfaction of work they enjoy.

More older people would like to continue some sort of employment than are able to at the present time.[17] In this respect, Alice has been very fortunate.

The oldest of six children, Alice grew up on a farm. Her father, an industrious man who lived to be eighty-four, wanted Alice to be a teacher and helped her go to college. She began teaching, but gave it up when she married, to work in her husband's business.

At forty years of age, Alice unexpectedly became pregnant. She and her husband had always wanted children, but had been told by their physician that they could not have any. Alice "retired" to become a full-time mother to a beautiful baby girl. This, her third "career," lasted fifteen years.

When her daughter was well along in high school, Alice bought a small shop that she enjoyed running until her husband died. This was a hard blow. She sold the shop and took a while to think about her future.

Then, at a time when most people retire, Alice found a job as a weekend relief telephone operator at a nearby hospital. Now at seventy-eight, her "retirement job" puts Alice in touch with people, gives her the satisfaction of serving her community, and yet its demands are not burdensome.

Not everyone is able to find the freedom and meaning in retirement as Vivian and Alice have. If the decision to retire is imposed by illness or employer policy it may be unwelcome. Feelings of bitterness or helplessness may result. When this is the case, pastoral care can enable the person to explore alternatives and experiment with a new lifestyle.

Even when retirement is welcomed, there may be some unanticipated complications. The pastor should not underestimate the significance of the shift from employment to retirement. Well-intentioned friends, and even retirees themselves, may fail to appreciate the impact of the changes which retirement brings.

"Retirement shock" may result from the sense of loss in a person who has strong ties to his or her work, and has found in it a sense of meaning and identity. Harried middle-aged or younger friends, whose image of retirement is that of an unending vacation, are likely to envy their retired friend's independence from schedules and deadlines. They may, therefore, overlook the mixed feelings of the retiree, expressing their assumptions in such remarks as "Now that you have so much time on your hands, how about helping me with this volunteer work?" or "Well, I'll bet you are really enjoying having time to catch up on your golf, now that you are your own boss!"

The pervasive changes which retirement or relocation can bring are graphically described by Sarah Patton-Boyle in an autobiographical account titled, *The Desert Blooms.*[18] Eagerly, and somewhat naively, she sought to make a new beginning in retirement.

She had enjoyed homemaking, but after her husband left and her children were grown, she decided to move from a college town to the suburbs of Washington, DC, to begin a new life.

She was not prepared for the shock that awaited her. At first, she was busy decorating her apartment to her own taste and exploring the shopping centers, art galleries, parks, and churches. She felt like a jack-in-the-box suddenly released.[19]

Within a few months, however, she made a painful discovery: "My luxurious sense of freedom to do what I choose when I choose was gone! Far from plunging into painting and writing, as I had expected, I felt immobilized."[20] The demands of outside pressures from which she had previously escaped through her writing were no longer there, but she faced a new bondage: "the weight of petty decisions."

It was natural for Patton-Boyle to turn to her church in this crisis. She had been a life-long Christian. She did, in fact, find friends in the church fellowship, including the pastor and his wife. But despite the helpfulness of many in the church, she found that even there the pain of her personal struggle was only dimly perceived. Her experience clearly shows that we cannot assume that retirement is pure joy. There may be joys, but it is also hard work.

In caring for people like Patton-Boyle, the pastor's task is to affirm the freedom of the retiree, while remaining alert to the possibility of "retirement shock." If her pastor had realized how helpless Patty felt, he or she might have intervened more effectively in her struggle to build a new life. Challenging the "young old" to find new ways to care for the world, the community, and other persons will forestall stagnation, loneliness, and self-pity.

*Advocacy and Support: Caring with Frail Seniors*

Of all people over sixty-five, only about 20 percent report having to limit their activities because of impaired health.[21] However, at some point in the aging process, health problems are likely to create concern. When they are severe enough to threaten continued independent living, advocacy and support are called for.

It is not unusual for older people to allude to their health concerns during pastoral calls. Such concerns should be taken seriously. If the person has not had medical attention recently, he or she may be encouraged to consult the family doctor. The studies mentioned above suggest that the pastor should be alert to a discrepancy between the health assessment of older people themselves and that of their physicians. Some people minimize serious problems, while others dramatize minor ones. The pastor may want to ask the person's permission to confer with the family doctor, or make a referral to a comprehensive geriatric evaluation clinic for assessment and recommendation. Such a clinic, usually available in major medical centers, can be helpful in dealing with more complex or puzzling health-related problems.

Ellen and Howard's story illustrates the themes of advocacy and support. When Howard was fifty-eight, anticipating retirement, they bought several acres of land on the outskirts of town and built a house, doing much of the work themselves. It was to be their last move. For twenty years they were very happy there.

Then, two years ago, Howard had a stroke. He is mentally alert, but limited in mobility. He gets about some by using a walker. Ellen, at seventy-four, continues in good health, and takes good care of Howard. However, she does not drive and so now both of them are pretty much confined at home.

Both their children are married. Their daughter lives about five hours away, and their son—a career Navy officer—is stationed in another state.

For many years, they were active members of their church. Ellen sang in the choir. Howard was a deacon and Sunday school teacher. Since Howard's stroke, they can no longer attend. However, they have kept up many of their ties. They send their offering and they welcome visitors from the church.

Now, in addition to Howard's stroke, a new turn of events has occurred that further threatens them. A developer acquired all the land surrounding their property and plans to build a shopping center. He offered a generous price for their place. The pastor made a call as soon as he heard the news. He listened as they shared their feelings.

Ellen, looking out the window at her garden, said, "I put out three new roses last year. When the dry weather came, I saved dishwater and took it out to keep them alive . . . but now, well . . . it's all gone."

Howard, his eyes filling with tears, said, "I feel like I'm losing everything I've worked for all these years. We have loved this place and thought we'd be right here until we died. I can't do much myself anymore, but I can enjoy what we did together . . . and our neighbors, how can we leave them? I just don't feel like starting over at my age!'"

How can advocacy and support be given to Howard and Ellen? Several possibilities come to mind. They can be summarized in three points: (1) provide continuity in a time of change, (2) mobilize a support system for extending independence, and (3) share in the task of life review.

As this couple anticipates the loss of their home, and with it a cherished identity, the immediate crisis is one of grief. The pastor's first instinct, to listen, will help them to grieve. Listening is supportive.

Howard and Ellen can't just grieve, however. They have to move, but the question is *where?* The pastor can help them explore alternatives for the next chapter in their lives. Should they stay in this community, or move nearer one of their children? Should they consider entering a retirement community which offers the possibility of life time care, if Howard's condition should change?

More is involved in moving than simply a choice among housing options. Howard and Ellen want to find a place where they can continue the pursuits that have given their lives meaning. The pastor helps them rank the options in terms of their life-long values, and may serve as an advocate for their right to make decisions for themselves.

During this time of tumultuous change for Howard and Ellen, the pastor can provide a point of continuity between their cherished past and an uncertain future. Their faith is a resource for them, as it was for Sarah Patton-Boyle.

In her essay referred to earlier in this chapter, Sarah Patton-Boyle describes the gulf between life as she had known it and her new life. She felt a deep need for "one area of stability, one unaltered link" with her past: "In the bewildering brokenness of my patterns of living, the church alone stood steady and unaltered, reaching back into my earliest childhood—a visible, touchable, long-remembered expression of my faith and a steadfast symbol of the unchanging love of God."[22] The pastor symbolizes that faith and love, and tries to incarnate it in relationships with the frail elderly.

In this enterprise, the pastor is not alone. In addition to personal caring, he or she can help to mobilize an appropriate support system for helping the frail elderly to maintain independent living for as long as possible. (Refer to the guiding assumptions noted earlier concerning family involvement and mobilizing the available resources, especially the case of Arnold.)

For Howard and Ellen, a support system might entail several elements. Their children would need to be considered. They might welcome sensitive guidance as to how they can best be supportive of their parents while still respecting their dignity and autonomy. Various resources of the church, such as the homebound program of the Sunday school, or tape ministry might be appropriate. Depending upon the sort of location Howard and Ellen choose, community services could be utilized. The main point here is that the pastor continues offering personal support while at the same time seeing that the resources of family, church, and community are coordinate.

Another way the pastor can support Howard and Ellen is by sharing with them in a process of life review. Some years ago, Robert Butler called attention to this phenomenon, which has received considerable attention in the literature of gerontology.[23] Butler pointed out that reminiscence, often viewed negatively as "living in the past," could serve a constructive purpose for older people, if they had a sensitive partner. Life review is a developmental task faced not only by older people, but by those of any age who anticipate death. It is an effort to separate the grain of life from its chaff. The pastor, or a trusted friend who is a good listener, can become a partner in this quest for meaning.

The clue to the possible utility of life review in the case of Howard and Ellen lies in Howard's feeling of helplessness. Ellen seemed a bit more flexible as she faced this transition. At one point she said to the pastor, "It's funny how things work out—seems to prepare you over the years for what's next." Although she shared Howard's grief, Ellen seemed hopeful.

Howard, by contrast, found it difficult to deal with relocating. He did not feel able to "start all over again," so he saw no future for himself. Having planned to die here, it is almost as though if he leaves, his life will be over. Life review may be a way of helping Howard to get in touch with his essential identity, which has roots much further back in his life than his ownership of this particular piece of real estate.

The physical task of moving will evoke many memories. Howard and Ellen will have to separate the keepsakes and heirlooms from the junk they have collected. In the process, they may gain a new perspective on their life story if they have the attention of an empathic listener. The listener's role is to look for continuity, for patterns, and above all for enduring meanings. To lift these up, to affirm them, and to understand the associated feelings, is a rewarding pastoral experience, and could help Howard find new purpose in his remaining years.

Life review may take various forms. Writing or taping autobiographies is perhaps the most obvious. Another idea might be to make a scrapbook of old photographs and clippings for one's children. Sometimes suggesting that a younger family member take a life history of a grandparent can result in important family communication.

Whatever its form, the goal of the life review is what Erikson described as the central developmental task of aging, the achievement of a sense of integrity, of "rightness" about one's life, rather than a sense of despair and defeat.

Ultimately, life review should free one to deal with the present. An Old Testament illustration comes from Isaiah. His encouragement to Israel in Babylon begins with a reminder of God's help at the Red Sea, when they were trying to escape an earlier captivity:

> Long ago the Lord made a road through the sea,
> a path through the swirling waters . . .
> But the Lord says,
> "Do not cling to events of the past
> or dwell on what happened long ago.
> Watch for the new thing I am going to do.
> It is happening already—you can see it now!
> I will make a road through the wilderness
> and give you streams of water there."[24]

Howard's reflection should help him to "watch for the new thing" that the Lord may be doing in his life.

"Good memories can be refreshing," notes Patton-Boyle, "and bad ones can be learned from." But, good or bad, when memories hamper present functioning, it is time to turn them out."[25]

As we have seen, most "younger" senior adults, and many of the "frail elderly," are relatively well and active. However, no treatment of pastoral care with senior adults would be complete without recognizing the needs of those who are coping with physical and mental impairments. We turn now to this concern.

### Respect and Closeness: Caring with Impaired Seniors

Sometimes health problems of later life leave senior adults with various degrees of impairment. The central themes in caring with impaired seniors are respect and closeness. The isolation that can result from physical, sensory, or mental impairment calls for pastoral initiative in overcoming the barriers to communication and in supporting personal dignity.

Familiar examples of limitations faced by some older people are the gradual loss of mobility from arthritis and the sudden paralysis from stroke. Having to depend on others to meet one's personal needs requires an adjustment that is difficult for many seniors.

If the impairment should result in disfigurement, as sometimes happens in the facial paralysis following stroke, a person may feel shame. Embarrassment may be felt also by older people as a result of incontinence. As a result of such experiences some persons may be tempted to withdraw from social contacts.

Caregivers with impaired seniors can do much to offset withdrawal if they convey a genuine respect which takes into account the total person, not just the visible impairment. Family, friends, and pastors who know the person's history are in a good position to communicate respect.

Two ways we can show respect are by affirming a person's right to privacy and decision making. A space of one's own and for personal "stuff," including significant memorabilia, is a tangible expression of respect.

Since impairments reduce the amount of control persons have over so much of their lives, whatever can be done to respect their

wishes and to give them choices is helpful. I remember with gratitude when this happened to my sister. She had just entered a nursing
home. She wanted to be cooperative, but for some reason she didn't
enjoy the worship service on Sunday afternoon. It was a relief and a
reassurance to her when the director of the home said to her, "If you
don't want to go, just stay in your room. Everybody needs something to say *no* to!"

Sensory handicaps may not be quite so visible as physical impairments, but they may be just as challenging both for the senior
adult and for the caregivers. In midlife we get a distant early warn-
ing of visual changes when we put on bifocals. The aging ear may
also lose some of its responsiveness to sounds of higher frequencies.

Older adults who have poor eyesight or hearing may tend to
avoid situations in which they feel inadequate or left out. Much can
be done, however, by caregivers, to enhance communication and
reduce isolation. Be alert to the indications of impairment in the
senior adults you visit. If a person wears glasses, but doesn't have
them on, ask if he or she would like to have them. If hearing is
better in one ear than another, try to speak toward the good side.
Speak distinctly, in lower tones, not necessarily louder. Occasionally, what appears to be apathy or confusion is greatly reduced when
people can hear or see what is going on.

Of all the impairments of later life, perhaps none is as greatly
feared or so baffling to family and friends as the mental handicap
known as dementia. Once regarded as the inevitable consequence of
old age, mental confusion among older people is now understood to
be the result of disease.

We now know that most impairment in the mental functioning of
older people results from Alzheimer's disease, a progressive loss of
thinking ability for which at present there is no cure. It often first
appears as a memory disorder, as when a person becomes disori-
ented in previously familiar surroundings. Because mental confusion can result from many causes, some of which are reversible, the
family of a confused older person should be urged to secure a
careful medical evaluation of their loved one.

As Alzheimer's disease progresses, family caregivers are subject
to severe emotional and physical stress. The victim may have a
tendency to wander, to be up at all hours of the night, and to require

around-the-clock attention. A helpful resource for family members is the guidebook, *The 36-Hour Day*, by Nancy L. Mace and Peter V. Rabins.[26] Local support groups offer help to family caregivers. For the address of local chapters, write to Alzheimer's Disease and Related Disorders Association, Inc., 360 N. Michigan Ave., Chicago, IL 60601.

Dementia reduces the person's capacity for abstract thinking. What this means for caregivers is that more attention must be given to the feeling side of communication. Caregivers who focus on the feelings of their loved one often discover a special kind of closeness which gratifies both the older person and the caregiver.

Two avenues are still open for communicating in spite of confusion. One is verbal and the other nonverbal. The verbal route consists of efforts to talk with the impaired person in an effort to discover the meaning in what may at first seem to be nonsense. This requires us to think in symbolic terms, and to hear more of the feelings being expressed, rather than worry over logical inconsistencies.[27]

For example, when my wife's mother says to us, "I don't know why Mac has been gone so long. I think he was taking a load of furniture to Lenoir," we don't fret over the fact that Mac, her husband, died in 1977. We don't tell her he'll soon be back. We focus on her feeling, which seems likely to be loneliness or grief. "Have you been missing Mac?" we may ask, or we may say, "It has been a long time since you saw him, so you wish he were here."

Family members who watch their loved one's memory slowly dwindling away are already having to mourn while the person is still alive. They may feel helpless and frustrated because they can't make things better.

A change in perspective has helped some caregivers feel less defeated. They stop trying to hold back the inevitable. They redefine their relationship to their loved one. Instead of seeing themselves as givers and their loved ones as weak, they put themselves into the role of learners. Instead of working for a certain response, they learn to enjoy the spontaneous response of their loved one to the simple joys of the moment—the beauty of a flower, the smile of a child.

One family member who changed her way of relating made a further reassuring discovery about her cousin: "his character and personality were unaltered by his dissolving ability to think. Although he no longer knew who anyone was, he related to all persons with courteous charm . . . he knew instantly when he was loved."[28]

Nonverbal forms of communication can be helpful in relating to individuals who have difficulty in understanding verbal messages. A wave of the hand, a smile, a warm handclasp, or a hug can convey friendliness, affection, and closeness when words fail.

Physical touch is the most powerful form of nonverbal communication. Although it should not be overused, or abused, it can often make contact when other means fail. It is usually welcomed if it is appropriate to the degree of closeness felt in the relationship.[29]

## CONCLUSION

At the beginning of this chapter, I mentioned two of my friends who taught me something about what it means to retire. Now at its conclusion, I am aware that they are only two of a much larger number of senior adults who have been my mentors. My experience with some of them is shared here. I take this opportunity to express my gratitude to them.

My experience has confirmed Henri Nouwen's insight that caring with the aging begins by allowing the aging to care for us. "When in careful listening we lift up the story of one person into the larger story of mankind," he notes, "we also connect the human story with God's story."[30]

While we can learn from all with whom we minister, only senior adults have the wisdom that comes from their years of life. As we share the journey of those who are moving toward the light, our own faith is increased, and we sense anew God's purpose for us for all our days—to glorify God and to declare His love to the world.

## NOTES

1. Zechariah 14:7, KJV.

2. Neugarten, Bernice L. "Personality Change in Late Life: A Developmental Perspective." *The Psychology of Adult Development and Aging*, Ed. Carl Eisdorfer and M. Powell Lawton. Washington, DC: American Psychological Association, 1973.

3. Havighurst, Robert J. *Developmental Tasks and Education*, Third Edition. New York: David McKay Co., 1972.

4. Ibid.

5. Duvall, Evelyn M. *Family Development*, Third Edition. Philadelphia: J. P. Lippincott, 1967.

6. Erikson, Erik H. *Childhood and Society*, Second Edition. New York: W. W. Norton, 1963.

7. _____, Ed. *Adulthood*. New York: W. W. Norton, 1978.

8. Ibid.

9. Peck, Robert C. "Psychological Developments in the Second Half of Life." *Middle Age and Aging*, Ed. Bernice L. Neugarten. Chicago: University of Chicago Press, 1968.

10. Ecclesiastes 12: 3-5. *Good News Bible*.

11. Koenig, Harold G. and Andrew J. Weaver. *Counseling Troubled Older Adults*. Nashville: Abingdon Press, 1997, p. 15.

12. Koenig, Harold G., Tracy Lamar, and Betty Lamar. *A Gospel for the Mature Years*. Binghamton, New York: The Haworth Press, Inc., 1997, p. 14.

13. Kerr, Horace. *How to Minister to Senior Adults in Your Church*. Nashville: Broadman Press, 1980, p. 73.

14. Brody, Elaine M. "Aged Parents and Aging Children." *Aging Parents*, Ed. Pauline K. Ragan. Los Angeles: University Press, 1989. Also, Shanas, Ethel. "The Family As a Social Support System in Old Age." *The Gerontologist*, 19 (1979), 169-174.

15. Westerhoff, John H. and William H. Willimon. *Liturgy and Learning Through the Life Cycle*. New York: The Seabury Press, 1980, pp. 149-152.

16. Kerr, p. 61.

17. Palmore, Erdman. "Facts on Aging: A Short Quiz," *The Gerontologist*, 17 (1977), 318.

18. Patton-Boyle, Sarah. *Desert Blooms*. Nashville: Abingdon Press, 1983, p. 26.

19. Ibid.

20. Ibid.

21. Palmore, *The Gerontologist*, 17 (1977), 317.

22. Boyle, p. 49.

23. Butler, Robert N. "The Life Review: An Interpretation of Reminiscence in the Aged," *Psychiatry*, 26 (1963), 65-76.

24. Isaiah 43: 16, 18-19. *Good News Bible*.

25. Boyle, p. 143.

26. Mace, Nancy L. and Peter V. Rabins, *The 36-Hour Day*. Baltimore: The Johns Hopkins University Press, 1981.

27. Meiburg, Albert L. "Pastoral Communication with the Confused," *Pastoral Psychology*, 31 (Summer 1983), 277.

28. Boyle, p. 190.

29. Meiburg, *Pastoral Psychology*, 31 (Summer, 1983), 274.

30. Nouwen, Henri J. J. "Care and the Elderly." *Aging and the Human Spirit*, ed. Carol LeFevre and Perry LeFevre. Chicago: Exploration Press of the Chicago Theological Seminary (1981), 291-296.

## ANNOTATED BIBLIOGRAPHY

Bianchi, Eugene C. *Aging As a Spiritual Journey.* New York: Crossroads, 1982.

A professor of religion at Emory University describes the human spiritual issues of middle-age and aging from a broadly Christian perspective. A classic of enduring value.

Boyle, Sarah-Patton. *The Desert Blooms: A Personal Adventure in Growing Old Creatively.* Nashville: Abingdon Press, 1983.

An artist and writer shares her story of relocation and retirement and how she overcame the resulting depression.

Burnside, Irene. *Working with the Elderly: Group Process and Techniques*, Second Edition. Monterey, CA: Wadsworth Health Sciences, 1984.

A distinguished nurse educator offers in-depth guidance for group work with older people,including reminiscence groups.

Clements, William M., ed. *Ministry with the Aging.* San Francisco: Harper and Row, 1981.

A text on ministry with older persons that has had long usefulness. Includes chapters on biblical and theological perspectives on aging.

Gwyther, Lisa P. *You Are One of Us: Successful Clergy/Church Connections to Alzheimer's Families.* Durham, NC: Duke University Medical Center, 1995.

Practical suggestions from the nationally known Duke Center for Aging Family Support Program. (919) 660-7510.

Kerr, Horace L. *How to Minister to Senior Adults in Your Church.* Nashville: Broadman, 1980.

A noted educator offers a practical plan for developing a church program for senior adults tailored to congregational needs.

LeFevre, Carol and Perry, eds. Aging and the Human Spirit: A Reader in Religion and *Gerontology.* Chicago: Exploration Press, Chicago Theological Seminary, 1981.

A rich collection of papers on aging from distinguished authorities in religion and social science, such as Abraham Heschel, Seward Hiltne, Ethel Shanas, Charles Longino, Dan Blazer, Erdman Palmore, and Henri Nouwen.

Koenig, Harold G. and Andrew J. Weaver. *Counseling Troubled Older Adults: A* Handbook for Pastors and Religious Caregivers. Nashville: Abingdon Press, 1997.

The director of the program on Religion, Aging, and Health of the Duke University Center for the Study of Aging and an ordained Methodist minister and clinical psychological collaborate in this handy guide to counseling elders with mental disorders. Case histories introduce each chapter and give clarity to the discussion.

Koenig, Harold G., Tracy Lamar, and Betty Lamar. *A Gospel for the Mature Years: Finding Fulfillment of Knowing and Using Your Gifts.* Binghamton, NY: The Haworth Pastoral Press, 1997.

Dr. Koenig teams up with a retired Episcopal priest and his wife to prepare this user-friendly study guide designed to challenge senior adults to discover God by discovering God's unique gifts to them.

Lapsley, James N. *Renewal in Late Life Through Pastoral Counseling.* Mahwah, NJ: Paulist Press, 1992.

An "age-inclusive model" for counseling elders focusing on the spirit and self, together with practical techniques, is offered by a distinguished pastoral theologian who served on the faculty of Princeton Theological Seminary for over thirty years.

Laslett, Peter. *A Fresh Map of Later Life: The Emergence of the Third Age.* Cambridge, MA: Harvard University Press, 1991.

In his sixties and seventies, Peter Laslett, a fellow of Trinity College, Cambridge, discovered the Third Age. Writing from experience in Britain, the author urges all people to plan for fulfillment in the years after sixty.

Lyon, K. Brynolf. *Toward a Practical Theology of Aging.* Philadelphia: Fortress Press, 1985.

Retrieving the ancient Christian traditions on aging, Brynolf challenges the secular idea of "fulfillment," and suggests the themes of hope, blessing, and redemption as guides for pastoral care in later life.

Maclay, Elise. *Green Winter: Celebrations of Old Age.* New York: Reader's Digest Press, McGraw-Hill, 1977.

Poetic word portraits of real people who are struggling with the issues of aging, and discovering the gifts of God in the process.

Meiburg, Albert L. "Pastoral Communication with the Confused." *Pastoral Psychology*, 31:4 Summer, 1983.

How caregivers can overcome the barriers presented by memory loss and confusion.

———— . "Pastoral Care with Older Adults." *Review and Expositor*, 88:3 Summer, 1991.

How caregiver perceptions of aging can hinder or enhance pastoral care with elders.

Stagg, Frank. *The Bible Speaks on Aging.* Nashville: Broadman Press, 1981.

A unique book, in that it looks at what the Bible says about aging, book by book. A much-loved New Testament scholar discovers things we have overlooked which can help us guide our experience of aging.

# Chapter 7

# Toward a Holistic Approach to Caring

## James E. Hightower Jr.

This book divided people into age groups, and the authors spoke to developmental tasks faced by persons from birth to death. Additionally, each author addressed how the spiritual life of a person develops from one life stage to the next.

Pastoral care would be much easier if it could be that cut and dried. Unfortunately it is not. Adults in the twilight years still deal with the issues of dependence/independence found in the preschool years. Likewise, adolescents are in some ways as much on the go as adults in their middle years.

This chapter will examine what it means to care, who is called to care, what skills are needed in caring, and pastoral care in time of crisis that transcends age or developmental task boundaries.

Persons need to be viewed as whole. Certainly we do pass through both chronological age and development task. But that is not the complete story.

## WHAT DOES IT MEAN TO CARE?

There are at least three qualities that people use in helping other persons. They are: accurate empathy, nonpossessive warmth, and genuineness.

### Accurate Empathy

Have you ever been with a friend for a brief period of time and known something was wrong? That's accurate empathy—feeling what someone else feels. Knowing that your friend hurts may be picked up in a multitude of ways.

- The person's voice may sound flat and depressed.
- The person may have a blank stare on his or her face rather than varied emotions.
- The person who is normally quiet may be agitated and unable to sit still.
- The person who is always on the go may be so still as to appear ill.
- How the person sits, looks at you (or doesn't look at you), or a hundred other ways are used to tell that something is wrong.

### Nonpossessive Warmth

In a conversation, my friend, Fred McGhee, defined nonpossessive warmth as "being able to respond with affection to the other person's need rather that using the other person to meet one's own need."

Pastoral counselors will be attuned to getting their personal needs met. However, these needs should be met by persons other than the hurt one with whom we are working. The pastoral counselor will build a support system in which his or her needs can be met. Pastors who counsel also need to find someone who can counsel them. It is not fair to a hurting person to bring my hurt into the counseling session.

Nonpossessive warmth is also caring for persons just as they are. Too often religious helpers give the impression that "I will care for you when (or if) you get your life back in order." The call to Christian helpers is to give warmth to persons whether they ever "get their life back in order again."

This idea of nonpossessive warmth is exemplified in Jesus of Nazareth. Jesus was in Jericho when He called a man named Zacchaeus down from a tree. Zacchaeus was the town's derelict. Everyone knew he was no good. People probably related to him in the "when you get your life straight, then we'll like you" mode. Everyone . . . except Jesus.

Jesus said, "Zacchaeus come down, I'm going to your house today." No strings attached; I'll care for you just like you are. In the warmth of fellowship and eating together Zacchaeus was converted. His conversion also led him to right his wrongs of the past.

People had tried the judgmental "if you do what we say, then we'll like you" method with Zacchaeus. Now the master showed the people of Jericho, and us, a new way. It is the way of nonpossessive warmth.

### Genuineness

Helpers will always have trouble here if they have a hard time accepting themselves. This element of caring is best described as sincerity. People who hurt need to know that the one who is helping them is real. Our model for genuineness is Jesus Christ, who related to people at all times with openness and honesty. We are called to follow Him as we learn to accept ourselves and to minister to others.

## WHO IS CALLED TO CARE?

The ministry of the Church is shared by all who name Jesus as Lord. This doctrinal view is called the priesthood of all believers.

We both have direct access to God and we are called to function as priests before God. A part of the priestly task is to care for persons. Pastoral ministry (caring for folks from birth to death) is more than a function for ordained clergy; it is every Christian's task.

Peter (2:4-10, NRSV) speaks clearly to us about our priesthood.

> Come to him, a living stone, though rejected by mortals yet chosen and precious in God's sight, and like living stones, let yourselves be built into a spiritual house, to be a holy priesthood, to offer spiritual sacrifices acceptable to God through Jesus Christ. For it stands in scripture: "See, I am laying in Zion a stone, a cornerstone chosen and precious; and whoever believes in him will not be put to shame."
>
> To you then who believe, he is precious; but for those who do not believe, "The stone that the builders rejected has become the very head of the corner," and "A stone that makes

them stumble, and a rock that makes them fall." They stumble because they disobey the word, as they were destined to do.

But you are a chosen race, a royal priesthood, a holy nation, God's own people, in order that you may proclaim the mighty acts of him who called you out of darkness into his marvelous light. Once you were not a people, but now you are God's people; once you had not received mercy, but now you have received mercy.

Verse 4 reminds us how we do ministry. As we "come to him" (Jesus Christ), we are enabled to do ministry. Ministry is done in the name of Jesus Christ; it is also done through Jesus Christ. Then the epistle writer tells us three aspects of this priesthood.

*We are called to be community.* In verse 5, the epistle writer gives us a new dimension to our faith in Jesus Christ. The gospel word is that Christians are always found in community.

You and I are living stones built into a spiritual house. That is where caring should always come from—the fellowship of believers.

Dietrich Bonhoeffer was one of the great Christians of our time. As a Nazi resister, he formed an underground seminary. For this special community, he wrote a discipline that is published under the title *Life Together.* The following is what he said about community in those extreme circumstances. "Christianity means community through Jesus Christ. No Christian community is more or less than this. Whether it be a brief, single encounter or the daily fellowship of years, Christian community is only this. We belong to one another only through and in Jesus Christ."[1]

The electronic church is a popular expression of present-day religious life in this country. However, this dimension of the contemporary religious scene cannot provide a sense of community like a local church.

*We are called to be priests.* The gospel word is that all Christians are priests. In the Old Testament only the priest had direct access to God. Then only the High Priest had access to God on the high holy day of the year. Then through Jesus Christ, the veil that separated the priest from the holy of holies was torn apart. You and I (clergy and laity alike) became priests who could function before God.

But what does a priest do? The Latin word for priest is *pontifex.* It means bridge builder. The priest is one who has access to God and whose task it is to bring others to God. The priest is a bridge builder.

The priest also brought the people's sacrifice to God. Paul gave this a new meaning for this new priest. Romans 12:1 declares, "Present your bodies as a living sacrifice, holy and acceptable to God, which is your spiritual worship" (NRSV).

Radical commitment is required. Once an animal brought to the priest would suffice. Now I must bring myself: my work, my family life, my relationships, my worship.

We who are New Testament priests are bridge builders between God and persons and person to person. Isn't that what pastoral care is? We have become God's own caring people. But we are God's people with a purpose. It is our individual privilege and our collective function as the church to care for persons. As we do this we praise God who called us from darkness to light.

Who is called to care? All Christians are ministers. That says to pastors who are called to "equip the saints for the work of ministry" (Ephesians 4:12, NRSV) that ways need to be developed to train laypeople in ministry. Reeducation is called for in this area so that when laypeople make a quality pastoral visit, it is identified as that by the pastor, the visitor, and the one visited.

## WHAT SKILLS ARE NEEDED TO CARE?

### Authentic Person

Remember Traux and Mitchell's three characteristics of a caring person? The third was genuineness. That's what I am talking about. The person who gives care must be perceived as being real. Sidney Jourard expressed it in these terms. "Authentic being means being oneself, honestly, in one's relations with his fellows. It means taking the first step at dropping pretense, defenses, and duplicity."[2]

The first skill we bring to caring for others is ourself. It is more than just bringing myself; it is bringing my real self with my joy, pain, pleasure, and suffering. It is bringing the me that is willing to let other people into my life. It is, as Henri Nouwen said, being a "wounded healer."

### Listening Person

In Bonhoeffer's discipline for the underground seminary, he wrote about the ministry of listening:

> The first service that one owes to others in the fellowship consists in listening to them. Just as love to God begins with listening to His Word, so the beginning of love for the brethren is learning to listen to them. It is God's love for us that He not only gives us His Word but also lends us His ear. So it is His work that we do for our brother when we learn to listen to him.[3]

My boyhood home was next to the Episcopal rectory. When my home church ordained me, my next door neighbor, the Episcopal rector, gave me two ordination gifts. One was the book titled *The Awesome Power of the Listening Ear* by John Drakeford. My Episcopal priest neighbor knew something I didn't know but needed to learn. Nothing in ministry beats listening!

Pastoral care is a congregational task. Laypersons are often ahead of their pastor in the caring skill of listening. Preachers are taught to be tellers, not listeners. Through the pastor's preaching/teaching ministry we are more interested in monologue than dialogue. Bonhoeffer's words need to be the preacher's theme. God, in love for us, gave us both Divine Word and Divine Ears. So how can you be a better listener? Let me enumerate several ideas.

### Give Your Full Attention to the One Who Is Speaking

Nothing substitutes for listening to a person. Listen to the verbal message, but also listen to the nonverbal message. What part of the story is so hard to describe that the person sounds as if he is chewing cotton? How is this person sitting or is she too nervous to sit for any length of time? What the person chooses not to say is often more important than what is said.

Listen also for voice-related clues. Perhaps part of a story is so hard to tell the person is on the verge of tears. Listen for joy-filled parts of the story that bubble out like a flowing brook. Listen for the flat, emotionless tone that denotes depression.

*Listen to the Feelings As Well As the Facts*
*of a Person's Story*

Hearing the facts (or the message) is only one half the task of a caregiver. The more important task is to hear a person's feelings. Is he feeling joy, depression, anger, guilt, regret, or some other emotion?

Let's say an adolescent comes to you and says: "I got so mad at my mother last night; I really told her off. I even told her to get out of my room and never come back."

The facts are a family fight. The feeling being talked about is anger. The feeling being expressed may be guilt or sorrow that comes in the guise of anger.

If the minister doesn't hear the deeper level expression, the teenager could well go away feeling unheard.

When a person gives care to another person, many feelings can be expressed in a short period of time. A major task of the counselor is to help the person focus on the dominate feelings.

*Be Aware of the Intensity of the Person Telling the Story*

Often the sheer intensity of the storyteller will be a vital clue to the minster.

If a person comes in with a story of horror in family relations and tells it with a smile, the counselor should beware. How do you tell horror stories and smile all the while? Perhaps the person hasn't allowed the awful reality to sink in yet.

Is the dominant feeling being expressed mild, moderate, or strong? Intensity tells you a great deal.

*Formulate a Response in Your Mind Before Answering*

Identify the content. Identify the dominant feeling. Then respond. A response to our hotheaded friend might be: "Are you feeling guilty over talking so harshly to your mother last night?"

## Let Your Tone Be Empathetic and Genuine

Let's stay with our teenage friend a minute. Remember how hard it was to declare your own personhood as a teenager? Recall those years before judging our young friend. That's what empathy is—trying to feel what someone else is feeling.

But also be genuine. As an adult it would be fine to let this teenager know you also understand his mother must be hurt. Don't deny the reality in order to make someone feel better. Yet, in facing reality, do it respectfully, not degrading the person.

## Check the Accuracy of Your Responses with the Person

You may have totally misread the situation. Give the person the right to tell you. Most people will give you several chances to hear their feelings before moving on to someone else.

Ask yourself the question: "Did my responses help this person explore the problem in a more helpful way?" If so, it was a good response.

## Barriers to Listening

Now we will look at some barriers to listening.

*Don't ask too many questions.* Allow persons to tell what they want you to know. Seldom does finding out more facts aid you in listening better.

*Don't finish people's thoughts for them.* It is humanly impossible to know precisely what another is going to say.

*Don't preach.* "Shoulds" and "oughts" only lead to barriers in listening to people. Believe that the Holy Spirit is powerful enough to work in each person's life. Allow the Spirit to guide this person.

*Don't deny the reality of feelings.* We've all had it happen. Someone comes to us feeling dumb. Our response is: "It's not true; you're one of the smartest people I know." That may be true; but if they're feeling dumb, they leave you feeling unheard or misunderstood.

*Don't be afraid of silence.* Silence can be a friend if we let it. Even if it is a defiant silence or a silence of withdrawing, it may be necessary for the person's sake. Silence can be creative.

*Don't listen just so you can tell your own story.* Listening to someone just so I can tell my story is not listening at all.

> I bend a sympathetic ear
> To other people's woes,
> However dull it is to know
> Their real or fancied throes.
> I pay to every gloomy line
> Attention undiminished.
> Because I plan to start on mine
> The moment theirs are finished.[4]

Seneca, the Roman poet, said:

> Listen to me for a day—an hour!—
> a moment! lest I expire in my ter-
> rible wilderness, my lonely silence!
> O God, is there no one to listen?

If you are going to care for people from birth to death, you will have to dedicate yourself to listening to them.

## PREACHING IS CARING

### Six Characteristics of a Caring Sermon

A sermon has a caring quality when:

*1. The preacher is perceived as a real human being.* A significant part of any sermon is the sermon deliverer. When the preacher is willing to share their humanity, the message will be more sincere. When the pastor must *act* like a plastic saint, the message will not be genuine. The preacher must give evidence that he or she is human with all the joys and hurts that entails.

*2. It answers questions people are asking.* The sermon should be grounded in Scripture but originated from human need. The sermon should reveal understanding of human need. When the preacher is a real person speaking to a real need the platform is set for a face-to-face encounter with God!

*3. It has given the congregation a chance to participate.* Persons learn through activity. Begin a Bible study group that helps you gain insight from the Scripture. Start a worship committee that aids in planning, implementing, and evaluating worshiP: Enlist lay leaders to help in the worship event.

Use different age groups. Children and teenagers can lead God's people in worship also. This is a signal to them, "My pastor thinks I'm a real person!" People learn best through activity, not passivity.

*4. It appeals to many senses.* One of the beauties of observing the Lord's Supper is that it can appeal to all five senses. The traditional sermon appeals to one sense (hearing) and in a limited way to sight. Each sense the pastor can add to the sermon makes a stronger caring sermon.

*5. It builds on past experience.* At times the wise pastor will lay extensive groundwork before preaching on a given issue. If a church has been plagued by conflict, the pastor will need to spend much time in relationship building, listening, and interpreting before publicly confronting the issue in a sermon.

Previous situations in an individual's or a community's life will affect learning. The wise pastor uses this to good advantage for the kingdom's sake.

*6. It helps persons meet their needs for security, mastery, and belonging.* Security will help persons build their self-esteem and affirm their worth in God's sight. Mastery will help persons see their lives in such a way that they are free to choose for or against God. Belonging will affirm the sense of community found in the local church. Belonging needs will also be met as the invitation is extended to join this household of faith.[5]

Caring is not complete until a new awareness of truth has broken through or until behavior has been changed. Preaching that is caring must be directed at enhancing a person's or community's knowledge or changing their behavior in the light of Jesus Christ.

## PASTORAL CARE IN TIMES OF CRISIS

Some crises of life transcend chronological age and/or developmental task. No one plans for these occasions; they happen. Two crisis events will be discussed here—hospitalization and grief. Other crisis events such as serious mental illness (major depression, bipolar, and schizophrenia) transcend age and developmental stages and are present in every congregation.

While skills will be emphasized in this section, the caring minister will always remember the developmental stage that the person is in.

Ministry to persons as individuals always takes into account who the person is and what stage of life they are in. Viewing persons as holistic beings also gives room for a person not to fit any theory of developmental stages.

### *Ministry to the Hospitalized*

The following is a pastoral conversation of mine as a beginning Clinical Pastoral Education student. It is not presented as model ministry, but as an example of ministry. C: represents the chaplain/minister, and P: represents the hospitalized patient.

The patient's first name was J. R. I was surprised to discover a woman in the room. I noticed the room had several bouquets of flowers and a fruit basket. It did not look like a room a person had occupied that afternoon. I made a mental note to check on how long she had been there.

As I entered, she was picking up the telephone to make a call. Responding to my knock, she said:

**P:** Come in.
**C:** Hello, Ms. M.?
**P:** Yes.
**C:** *(I began with a little chuckle and said)* When I saw the name J. R. I did not expect to find you—I've never heard J. R. as a woman's name before.
**P:** *(chuckling)* I know—that is not a common name—most people just don't admit it surprises them.
**C:** Well, let me introduce myself. I am Chaplain Hightower from the hospital. I wanted to visit you and see what is going on with you.
**P:** I'm glad you came by. You know I had a hysterectomy last week. I came through it just fine, with very little worry. Later that week they found a lump in my right breast—they X-rayed

me and the doctor said that lump was nothing, but found a mass in my left breast that he said must be tested. He may even do a radical. *(Her eyes begin to cloud up at this point.)* You know, I do not understand why I could go through the hysterectomy with no problem and I am scared to death of this operation in the morning.

**C:** How do you see the surgery tomorrow as being different from the surgery last week?

**P:** I am really afraid they will find something tomorrow that we cannot handle—with the hysterectomy it was routine. I'd just had some trouble and that was the easiest cure. I'm afraid they will find cancer and I'll die. *(At this point, the patient began to sob and in her sobbing looked at me—I reached my hand out to her and before my hand got to hers, she reached and met mine. This seemed to tell her that I understood her need to cry.)*

Then we begin talking about the fear of death and the possible results of the forthcoming surgery. The dialogue seemed to center on the fear of leaving a husband and two children behind instead of the fear of possible radical surgery. After a few minutes of this discussion, the conversation followed this course.

**C:** Ms. M., I hope you will find some new spiritual resources or be able to call on some old ones to help you face the anxiety before surgery and to face whatever the report may be tomorrow. I want you to know I will be praying for you as you face the events of tomorrow. *(Her look seemed to say let's do it now.)* Sometimes I pray with people in their room. Would you like this, or should I remember you later?

**P:** Let's pray now, please.

**C:** Dear Lord, I thank you for my new friend. I trust this friend and all her needs to your care. We acknowledge the fear of death but we also acknowledge our faith in you. Lord, we pray you will bless all involved in the events of tomorrow and especially do we pray you will bless those she loves so much. We are your children and we trust our cares into your hands. Amen.

**P:** I know I'll face this surgery with new faith. Thank you for coming.

**C:** God bless you. *(I left.)*

The next day, I checked with the chaplain on her floor and asked to go back up and see her.

Upon arriving on the floor, I checked with the nurse as to the outcome of the surgery. The report was negative, so the radical surgery was not done.

The head nurse overheard me asking, and she got up and came to the desk. She wanted to know if I was the chaplain who had spoken with Ms. M. last evening. I told her I was, and she thanked me for the time I spent with her. She said, "I heard you cried with her last night; now please go down and rejoice with her." I thanked the nurse and went to the patient's room.

> **C:** Hey, I hear you have good news.
> **P:** *(Smiling.)* I was hoping you would come by so I could tell you. Thank you so much for praying to God for me.
> **C:** I'm glad I got to meet you and share some of this experience with you. *(She then introduced me to her husband and mother. We talked briefly, then I left.)*

Several things strike me that I did correctly.

1. *I knocked before entering the room.* You must remember that a hospital room is both a living room and a bedroom. Depending on the patient's condition, it might be bathroom also. The patient's room is a private place. Don't enter before you knock.
2. *I was honest.* I was surprised to find a woman named J. R. I was genuine in saying so. The patient's response was: "Most people just don't admit it surprises them." That started us on an honest relationship.
3. *I identified myself.* Even if you are the pastor visiting a faithful member you've known for ten years, identify yourself. It is possible the person is so medicated as to be confused or has seen so many strangers coming in and out of the room, he simply does not recognize you.

Be careful how you identify yourself. Don't use the academic title of *Doctor* in a hospital setting. I have a friend who was recently awarded his doctorate. He was so proud of it he used the title wherever he went. Soon after receiving the degree, he moved to a new pastorate. One of his first visits was to a female member of the church who was hospitalized. He had not previously met her. Upon entering the room he said, "I'm Dr. S_____."

The lady immediately said "Thank goodness, you're here. This incision is driving me crazy." Her subsequent action was intended for a doctor, not her new pastor. Needless to say my friend was embarrassed, and his new church member was humiliated.

Identify yourself as a minister, not as "Doctor so and so."

4. *I let the patient express her emotions.* She was visibly upset and she had a right to be. I let her know by a simple touch that it was permissible to cry in my presence. I also allowed her to use two words that are taboo in our culture—death and cancer. For J. R., naming the monster gave her some control over it.

5. *I let the patient take the lead in discussing her problem.* I made an open-ended comment. "I wanted to visit with you and see what is going on with you." That let her take the lead with the conversation. It put her in the control position.

6. *I helped her call on her own spiritual resources.* This was done by acknowledging her need for prayer.

It should be noted that the follow-up the next day was an important part of the pastoral visit. Dennis E. Saylor in his book—*And You Visited Me!* offers these twelve suggestions for hospital ministry:

1. Knock before entering a patient's room.
2. Walk and talk softly.
3. Shake hands only at the patient's request.
4. Have a pleasant facial expression.
5. Be brief.
6. Visit the patient when you are well.
7. Remember that the patient's condition is personal.
8. Consider the patient's rights.
9. Keep personal problems to yourself.
10. Maintain eye contact.
11. Always identify yourself.
12. Enter the room only if the call light above the door is not on.[6]

Hospitalization happens to persons of all ages. It is a life accident that transcends chronological age or developmental task. It is more often than not viewed as a crisis time for persons. Therefore, ministers are rightly expected to be expert at hospital ministry.

One word needs to be said about children in the hospital. When a child is hospitalized, the minister should visit the child, not just the parents. The pastor should leave the room with that child knowing he or she is special.

The minister should never underestimate the value of personal presence. Far more valuable than saying the right words or picking up on the person's cues is being there.

Jesus' words "and you visited me" are not to be taken lightly. Physical presence is a major part of caring for folks from birth until death.

### Ministry to the Grieving

From birth to death we are grievers. Life might well be defined as a series of mini-griefs interspersed with major grief. We normally associate grief with someone's death. "Her husband died and she is grieving," we say. Yet this woman has known many mini-griefs before this time. What are some of them that she and other persons face?

Leaving her parent's home to attend college or to marry was a grief experience for both her and her parents. It was the death of one relationship (or at least its reconstruction) and the birth of a new one.

The birth of a child, particularly the first child, ushers in the death of one way of life and birth to a new way. Postpartum blues are in acknowledgment of that grief, as well as a physical imbalance helped by medical attention and medication. Some other examples follow:

- The loss of a job is most often a major grief.
- Buying a home can cause anxiety over the financial responsibility, and it can herald a new era of responsibility.
- Moving from a beloved city to another city or a beloved house to a new residence can be a source of grief.

- The failure of significant plans for one's job, security, family, or parents can cause grief.
- An illness or hospitalization can cause us to grieve over our mortality and/or our declining physical powers.

You can list occasions of grief in your own life. Any loss causes physical and emotional reactions that we call grief.

## Five Stages in the Grief Process

*On Death and Dying*[7] is a significant work in which Elisabeth Kübler-Ross traced five discernable stages in the grief process. These are descriptive rather than scientifiC: They are also spirals rather than linear stages.

### Denial and Isolation

This is the feeling "No, not me; it cannot be true." Denial is used by virtually everyone. I believe it should be seen as a gift from God. It allows us to protect ourselves from tragic news until we can muster courage to hear it. A feeling of loneliness and isolation is also very prevalent during this stage.

### Anger

The anger stage asks the question "Why me?" The first stage of denial cannot be maintained any longer so it is replaced by feelings of rage, resentment, and anger. Often this anger is given to family members, employers, doctors, nurses, ministers. It is a way of saying: "I'm not finished yet; you have to listen to me."

### Bargaining

If anger has not worked to take away our hurt, then perhaps asking politely will. We learn as children that asking nicely gets one further with parents than demanding. In the bargaining stage we ask

God politely, "God, if I become a preacher will you get me out of this mess?" or "God, I'll never hit my wife again if you'll make her come back to me." Bargaining is often filled with irrational fears and excessive guilt.

## Depression

When the person realizes the great loss he or she has sustained, then depression sets in. For the terminally ill person this depression may be a form of preparatory grief where impending loss is prepared for. It is a tool used to prepare more easily. Whether grief is due to a situational loss or a preparation to die, the person should be allowed to be depressed—to mourn the loss.

## Acceptance

This is not a happy state; rather it is almost devoid of feeling. It is a signal that the struggle is over. It is the woman who can say: "I lost a breast to cancer." It is the man who can say: "After thirty-four years with the company, I lost my job."

Kübler-Ross did not say we go through these stages sequentially so that stage 1 leads to stage 2, and so forth. Rather, a person can be in acceptance today (or this hour) and in denial the next day (or next hour). Grief is a journey with crooked roads and many turn-back signs; it is not an interstate highway connecting two points at the shortest distance.

Persons grieve regardless of chronological age or developmental task. The preschool child who loses a pet grieves. The middle-age child who moves from one town to another grieves. The adolescent who loses a first "love" to another girl or boy grieves. The young adult who doesn't get the job hoped for grieves. The adult whose child leaves home grieves. The older adult grieves failing health or loss of sight, hearing, or mobility.

From birth to death we are grievers. What can minsters do to care for persons who grieve?

1. *Ministers can be physically present.* In grief-education workshops, my most often asked question is: "What do you say to

someone who is grieving?" I do not believe a grieving person will remember what you say, unless it is so unfeeling as to offend them. What grieving people will remember is whether or not you were present with them.

2. *Ministers can listen.* Many pastors feel they are called to tell, not to listen. God's love is proven to us in that He gave us His Word to speak and His ear to listen. Listen to a person in both content and feelings. Often our own fear of grief will not permit us simply to sit with one who is grieving.

3. *Ministers can help mobilize a support system for the griever.* The church can express itself as an extension of God's love when people will risk caring.

4. *Ministers can be genuine.* If you are uncomfortable in the face of grief, acknowledge that feeling. Then find someone to help you work on it. The more comfortable you are in the face of grief, the more you will be able to minister to the grieving.

## SPIRITUALITY:
## A PERSONAL AND COMMUNAL JOURNEY

When *Caring* was originally written, I was thirty-three years old. Now I will mail this revision to the editor four weeks past my forty-eighth birthday. In 1983, I would not have written about the importance of a growing spirituality. Fifteen years later, it is too important not to write about.

Growth is no easier for the minister than it is for any other person. Spiritual growth is often equally tumultuous.

Growing is never easy. The child has leg cramps because growing is occurring too quickly. The youth continues to change majors in school because choosing any one major feels too final. Then perhaps goals are set for marriage, a family, career, finances, religious faith, and other areas. These are achieved or not achieved. For most of us it is a time of both success and failure. When all the growing that can be offered from youth is done, midlife blossoms. Along with it comes a unique call for continued growth. The following is what I am learning about being a minister in midlife.

First, I am going to die. Several years ago, I wrote a high school friend of mine a note because his cancer was no longer treatable.

We graduated together, and now he is dead. Recently, at a family gathering, I kissed a favorite cousin and said, "I'm much too young for you to be a grandmother." It was a bad stab at gallows humor.

Ironically this fresh knowledge of death is not depressing. It is a wake-up call to live life large. There is no more time for pettiness or other brands of smallness. Life is meant to be lived fully. Midlife is a time to expand our hearts so that other people and causes can have room.

Second, I am learning that life is best lived in chapters. Realizing I have reached midlife means a new chapter is beginning. I am grateful to my teacher-mentor, Elton Trueblood, for teaching me this lesson. Ironically, it was his death in December 1994 that made me realize that midlife for me is here. I have become the next generation.

I have been through the life chapters of student, denominational worker, and pastoral counselor in a local church. In those years I married Cathy, parented Brent and Lauren, wrote extensively, edited a journal, and served wonderful churches. Now is the beginning of something new. I am reinventing myself as a counseling center director and a counselor educator. I view this time (being an avid fiction reader) as the beginning of a new chapter in a good book. I don't know what it will reveal but I'm anxious to see.

The third lesson I'm learning is that I can have a good life despite not having accomplished my goals. Midlife has been a time of grief for me. I had really hoped to write a book, one that would make a great impact. (Remember, Trueblood was my mentor!) Out of the eight books published, the first edition of this is the only one that has been used in several seminaries and translated into Spanish. None have met my narcissistic expectations.

Career has had its grief also. Early on I was a fast tracker, beginning work with my denomination at the age of twenty-nine. Five years later, it was clear to me the denomination was irrevocably broken.

When I returned to a local church, the heartbeat of Baptists, I brought with me a grief-filled heart. Grief filled for friends who had been hurt or displaced. Grief filled for myself and my own displacement. Grief over my family's suffering because of their losses due to moving. Grief over my center of concern going from a national perspective to one city block and now to one long hallway in a hospital! These losses are immeasurable.

For most of us, a similar kind of loss of a dream occurs and always stings. Yet life can be good. Without the losses I would have spent a lifetime giving my life to a denomination. The loss has helped me reclaim my life. These experiences have all taught me a valuable lesson: All human institutions are subject to evil; only God deserves full loyalty.

So how is life good now?

I'm learning to enjoy the small things in life far more. A letter or phone call from or to a longtime friend becomes a celebration. A magazine article sold and published becomes a time to rejoice. Watching my children grow into their own persons is a time of real satisfaction.

I've also learned to trust my ability to survive the ups and downs of life more than when I was younger. I am more inclined now to watch and see what will happen rather than assume a crisis is around every corner. Life is not what I expected it to be; however, life is good.

The fourth thing I am learning in midlife is that accomplishment does not satisfy me like it once did. A life of ministry is an interesting one to live. One way it is interesting is that the number of church members you have is the number of supervisors you also have. (And some of these supervisors have multiple opinions on a single topic!) Earlier in ministry I wanted to please everyone. Most of you reading this reflection know how tiring that can be.

Recently, I've sensed a change that I've tagged "my internal compass." In midlife I am individuated enough from my external environment that what I think and feel is really important.

This leads me to my point—internal accomplishment is becoming more important than external accomplishments. Companionship with my wife that leads to a deep abiding friendship is more important than any writing project I could do. Maintaining friendships with people who have been close friends over the years will be more satisfying than one more speech given to any grouP: Knowing that I have done well by the elderly and young in my family is more valuable than one more "good" career move. Perhaps this "internal compass" that calls for balance is a type of wisdom only available to most of us in midlife and on.

The fifth thing I'm learning in midlife is very unpleasant. It is that for all of the good I've done in life (after all, I am a minister!), I have hurt a lot of people—the people that I love the most. Coming to terms with myself and my destructiveness is very painful. I could tell you stories about parents, career, children, and my destructiveness, but decency restrains me.

By midlife I had hoped to feel adequate. I'd hoped to be adequate in my marriage, in my career, and in my parenting. All these things are true and they must be laid beside my destructiveness in my marriage, in my career, and in my parenting.

At midlife I find myself a sinner in need of God's grace. This newfound sinfulness also leads me to the final awareness that I've learned about myself in midlife.

I have begun to yearn for a depth of spirituality not found in religious faith. A metaphor for my midlife years might well be the "desert." These desert years have led me to a group of monastics and the Rule of Saint Benedict.

Benedict was a sixth-century Christian more concerned with the practice of Christian faith than the theory of Christian faith. Benedict loved God and believed that the Christian life was best lived in Christian community. His Rule became a primary guide to monastic life that is still in use today.

The Benedictine way is about radical listening and radical hospitality. Benedictines practice radical listening through the Liturgy of the Hours as the Psalms are prayed and other scripture heard several times a day in the gathered community. This listening for God's voice also leads Benedictines to listen to those they serve and to listen to each other.

Benedictines practice private radical listening also, through the ancient practice of *Lectio Divina* (Divine Reading).

Four components compose this way of listening for the Divine:

1. *Lectio* (reading): Take a passage of Scripture or other devotional/theological work and read aloud a brief passage.
2. *Meditatio* (meditation): Allow a word or phrase to draw you as you meditate.

3. *Oratio* (prayer): Allow this divine word to penetrate your heart. A prayerful response might be a natural reaction.
4. *Contemplatio* (contemplation): Give this process back to the giver as you allow the Spirit to guide you.[8]

Then go on with what life calls you to.

This guide has helped Christians deepen their spiritual lives for fifteen hundred years. It is not a denominational program, a passing fad, or a way a religious publishing house can make money. It is free to the seeker.

Benedictines also practice radical hospitality. This grace gift is found first through finding oneself; the spiritual practice of humility. Our word humility comes from the Latin word "humus." Humus means "of or from the earth." A person who exercises the spiritual practice of humility is a person with both feet planted on the ground. They know who they are, both the good and the bad. This knowing and acceptance of oneself leads to humility.

Benedictines also practice the art of hospitality. In Chapter 53 of his Rule Benedict tells the guest master of the monastery: "All guests who present themselves are to be welcomed as Christ" (v.1).[9]

Today Benedictine communities are known for the open embrace of all who enter. As an Oblate (associate member) of Sacred Heart Monastery in Cullman, Alabama, each return is going home again.

That is what drew me to Benedict's way of doing the Christian life: radical listening and radical hospitality. In a day that is too hurried to listen and more expert at barrier building than radical hospitality, it has become my way of the spiritual life.

In no way would I say it should be your way. Rather, discovering your way to spiritual aliveness is what is important. At nearly fifty years of age, I know spiritual vitality is important.

## CONCLUSION

I have found that midlife holds its own wisdom. In midlife some things sacred to me earlier are dying or have died. In other places of my midlife, new life has burst through. At midlife I yearn for companionship with God and companionship with others more than ever before.

Benedictines make three vows: stability (to a house), obedience (that we owe God, our superiors and our equals), and fidelity (daily conversion to the way of Christ). For me, in midlife, these are three good vows.

## NOTES

1. Dietrich Bonhoeffer, *Life Together*, trans. John W. Doberstein. New York: Harper and Row, 1954, P: 21.
2. Sidney M. Jourard, *The Transparent Self*. New York: D. Van Nostrand Company, 1971, pP: 133-134.
3. Bonhoeffer, P: 97.
4. Norman Jeffray, "Good Listener," *Saturday Evening Post*, December 6, 1958, P: 40. Quoted in John Drakeford, *The Awesome Power of the Listening Ear*. Waco, TX: Word Books, 1967, P: 47. Used with permission of *The Saturday Evening Post*.
5. This section was adapted from a chapter I prepared in a book compiled by Will Beal, *I'm My Own M.E.!* Nashville: Convention Press, 1985.
6. Dennis E. Saylor, *—And You Visited Me*. Seattle: Morse Press, Inc., 1979, pP: 45-48.
7. Elisabeth Kübler-Ross, *On Death and Dying*. New York: The Macmillian Co., 1969.
8. *Benedictirie Oblate Companion*, 1997, Saint Meinrad Archabbey. St. Meinrad, IL.
9. *The Rule of St. Benedict in English*, Timothy Fry, OSB, editor. Collegeville, MN: The Liturgical Press, 1982, P: 73.

## ANNOTATED BIBLIOGRAPHY

Chittister, Joan D. *Wisdom Distilled from the Daily: Living the Rule of St. Benedict Today.* San Francisco, CA: Harper, 1990.

> Spiritual guidelines for everyday living taken from The Rule of St. Benedict in fifth century Rome.

Doka, Kenneth J. *Living with Grief After Sudden Loss: Suicide, Homicide, Accident, Heart Attack, Stroke.* Bristol, PA: Taylor and Francis, 1996.

> Another must read for ministers who care during all types of traumatic death. Produced for the Hospice Foundation of America. Call the Foundation at 1-800-854-3402 for details on ordering this book in bulk orders or 1-800-821-8312 for individual orders.

Fisher, Bruce. *Rebuilding When Your Relationship Ends*, Second Edition. San Luis Obispo, CA: Impact Publishers, 1996.

An excellent resource for use in church-related divorce recovery groups. Fisher outlines nineteen rebuilding blocks beginning with denial and ending with freedom. Special attention is given to children of divorce.

Friedman, Edwin H. *Generation to Generation: Family Process in Church and Synagogue*. New York: The Guilford Press, 1985.

Applying the concept of systemic family therapy using the congregation as a family.

Fry, Timothy. *The Rule of Benedict in English*. Collegeville, MN: The Liturgical Press, 1982.

This Rule for monastic life continues to be a living, breathing document after 1500 years.

Patton, John. *Pastoral Care in Context: An Introduction to Pastoral Care*. Louisville, KY: Westminister/John Knox Press, 1993.

Patton identifies three paradigms of pastoral care: the classical, the clinical pastoral and the communal contextual. In the communal contextual he clearly ties the work of caring as a ministry of the church rather than a ministry of just ordained clergy. This is a clear look at pastoral issues.

Sutera, Judith. *Work of God: Benedictine Prayer*. Collegeville, MN: The Liturgical Press, 1994.

A Benedictine religious has compiled a good beginning point for persons interested in Benedictine spirituality including two weeks of morning and evening prayer in the Benedictine tradition.

Switzer, David K. *The Minister As Crisis Counselor*; Revised and Enlarged. Nashville: Abingdon, 1987.

The definitive work on crisis counseling for the active minister. Included is a chapter on methods of crisis counseling and chapters on major crisis such as family crises, grief as crises, the minister and divorce crises and intervening in suicidal crises.

Woolis, Rebecca. *When Someone You Love Has a Mental Illness*. New York: Putnam Books, 1992.

This is a handbook for people coping with the daily issues of mental illness. It is a "must read" for all pastors who will deal with the effects of mental illness on their lives.

# Index

Page numbers followed by the letter "f" indicate figures.

# THE HAWORTH PASTORAL PRESS
Pastoral Care, Ministry, and Spirituality
Richard Dayringer, ThD
Senior Editor

**LOSSES IN LATER LIFE: A NEW WAY OF WALKING WITH GOD, SECOND EDITION** by R. Scott Sullender. "Continues to be a timely and helpful book. There is an empathetic tone throughout, even though the book is a bold challenge to grieve for the sake of growth and maturity and faithfulness.... An important book." *Herbert Anderson, PhD, Professor of Pastoral Theology, Catholic Theological Union, Chicago, Illinois*

**CARING FOR PEOPLE FROM BIRTH TO DEATH** edited by James E. Hightower Jr. "An expertly detailed account of the hopes and hazards folks experience at each stage of their lives. Your empathy will be deepened and your care of people will be highly informed." *Wayne E. Oates, PhD, Professor of Psychiatry Emeritus, School of Medicine, University of Louisville, Kentucky*

**HIDDEN ADDICTIONS: A PASTORAL RESPONSE TO THE ABUSE OF LEGAL DRUGS** by Bridget Clare McKeever. "This text is a must-read for physicians, pastors, nurses, and counselors. It should be required reading in every seminary and Clinical Pastoral Education program." *Martin C. Helldorfer, DMin, Vice President, Mission, Leadership Development and Corporate Culture, Catholic Health Initiatives—Eastern Region, Pennsylvania*

**THE EIGHT MASKS OF MEN: A PRACTICAL GUIDE IN SPIRITUAL GROWTH FOR MEN OF THE CHRISTIAN FAITH** by Frederick G. Grosse. "Thoroughly grounded in traditional Christian spirituality and thoughtfully aware of the needs of men in our culture.... Close attention could make men's groups once again a vital spiritual force in the church." *Eric O. Springsted, PhD, Chaplain and Professor of Philosophy and Religion, Illinois College, Jacksonville, Illinois*

**THE HEART OF PASTORAL COUNSELING: HEALING THROUGH RELATIONSHIP, REVISED EDITION** by Richard Dayringer. "Richard Dayringer's revised edition of *The Heart of Pastoral Counseling* is a book for every person's pastor and a pastor's every person." *Glen W. Davidson, Professor, New Mexico Highlands University, Las Vegas, New Mexico*

**WHEN LIFE MEETS DEATH: STORIES OF DEATH AND DYING, TRUTH AND COURAGE** by Thomas W. Shane. "A kaleidoscope of compassionate, artfully tendered pastoral encounters that evoke in the reader a full range of emotions." *The Rev. Dr. James M. Harper, III, Corporate Director of Clinical Pastoral Education, Health Midwest; Director of Pastoral Care, Baptist Medical Center and Research Medical Center, Kansas City Missouri*

**A MEMOIR OF A PASTORAL COUNSELING PRACTICE** by Robert L. Menz. "Challenges the reader's belief system. A humorous and abstract book that begs to be read again, and even again." *Richard Dayringer, ThD, Professor and Director, Program in Psychosocial Care, Department of Medical Humanities; Professor and Chief, Division of Behavioral Science, Department of Family and Community Medicine, Southern Illinois University School of Medicine*

# Order Your Own Copy of
# This Important Book for Your Personal Library!

## CARING FOR PEOPLE FROM BIRTH TO DEATH

_____ in hardbound at $39.95 (ISBN: 0-7890-0571-9)

COST OF BOOKS_____

OUTSIDE USA/CANADA/
MEXICO: ADD 20%_____

POSTAGE & HANDLING_____
*(US: $3.00 for first book & $1.25
for each additional book)
Outside US: $4.75 for first book
& $1.75 for each additional book)*

SUBTOTAL_____

IN CANADA: ADD 7% GST_____

STATE TAX_____
*(NY, OH & MN residents, please
add appropriate local sales tax)*

**FINAL TOTAL**_____
*(If paying in Canadian funds,
convert using the current
exchange rate. UNESCO
coupons welcome.)*

☐ **BILL ME LATER:** ($5 service charge will be added)
(Bill-me option is good on US/Canada/Mexico orders only;
not good to jobbers, wholesalers, or subscription agencies.)

☐ Check here if billing address is different from
shipping address and attach purchase order and
billing address information.

Signature_____

☐ **PAYMENT ENCLOSED: $**_____

☐ **PLEASE CHARGE TO MY CREDIT CARD.**

☐ Visa    ☐ MasterCard    ☐ AmEx    ☐ Discover
☐ Diner's Club

Account # _____

Exp. Date _____

Signature _____

Prices in US dollars and subject to change without notice.

NAME _____

INSTITUTION _____

ADDRESS _____

CITY _____

STATE/ZIP _____

COUNTRY _____ COUNTY (NY residents only) _____

TEL _____ FAX _____

E-MAIL_____
May we use your e-mail address for confirmations and other types of information? ☐ Yes    ☐ No

*Order From Your Local Bookstore or Directly From*
**The Haworth Press, Inc.**
10 Alice Street, Binghamton, New York 13904-1580 • USA
TELEPHONE: 1-800-HAWORTH (1-800-429-6784) / Outside US/Canada: (607) 722-5857
FAX: 1-800-895-0582 / Outside US/Canada: (607) 772-6362
E-mail: getinfo@haworthpressinc.com
PLEASE PHOTOCOPY THIS FORM FOR YOUR PERSONAL USE.

BOF96